LATHEWORK

A Complete Course

Harold Hall

SPECIAL INTEREST MODEL BOOKS

Special Interest Model Books Ltd.
Stanley House
3 Fleets Lane
Poole
Dorset
BH15 3AJ

First published by S.I.Model Books Ltd. 2003

Reprinted 2005, 2006.

© Special Interest Model Books Ltd. 2006

ISBN 1-85486-230-8
ISBN-13: 978-1-85486-230-3

Printed and bound in Malta by Progress Press Co. Ltd

Contents

Preface   7

Chapter 1   Getting started   9

Chapter 2   Mini surface gauge   17

Chapter 3   Precision square   35

Chapter 4   A between-centres test bar   45

Chapter 5   Hole gauges   51

Chapter 6   Distance gauges   59

Chapter 7   Tailstock die holders   69

Chapter 8   Precision tapers   81

Chapter 9   Screw jack   89

Chapter 10   Jack continued - screw cutting   99

Chapter 11   Getting to grips with the face-plate   111

Chapter 12   Mill drill spindle   129

Chapter 13   A milling cutter chuck   149

Preface

The main aim of this book is to take the newcomer to turning from the novice stage through to an experienced beginner, achieving this by providing a range of projects each one primarily illustrating a particular process. Finally the book concludes with two quite advanced projects that will put to the test the skills learnt in earlier chapters.

Having spent a short while as editor of *Model Engineers' Workshop*, I am also aware that many have limited time for workshop activity and these, even if experienced, will find the projects useful as most can be completed in a matter of a few hours. No doubt, some useful tips being gleaned from the book on the way even for the experienced turner.

Whilst just reading the book will provide the beginner with much useful information this will be a poor substitute to actually making the items described. The reader is therefore encouraged to at least make most of the items detailed.

Removing metal using a metal work lathe is a straightforward process with quality work being easily achievable. However, the range of processes possible make the task of coming to terms with operating a lathe quite an extensive course that this book aims to provide.

Using a milling machine is on the other hand quite the reverse with obtaining a presentable finish much more of a problem but with each task being much more like others carried out on the machine. In this case the main requirement is to spend time on the machine to feel at home with its capabilities. A follow-up book to this will address the requirement with a range of projects aimed at giving the necessary time spent using the machine.

Harold Hall, 2003

Chapter 1

Getting started

Prior to getting to grips with the projects in this book some discussion regarding the lathe and the accessories that go with it is included for the newcomer to turning.

The Machines

Of course a lathe is a necessity, though for some this may initially be a machine available at the local technical college. If you are purchasing a lathe for the first time it is difficult to advise, as it will depend on the type of work envisaged and what other machines are to be acquired, two points are thought worth emphasising. First, if space and funds are available purchase a lathe of at least 90mm bed to centre height and secondly purchase a lathe with a tee slotted cross slide. The last point is a must if the workshop will not have a milling machine and even if it has many simple milling operations are easier to perform on the lathe as is illustrated in Chapter 13 Photos 14 and 15. However, as the projects are primarily aimed at those with limited experience it is assumed that other activities, typically milling, are even more of an unknown quantity. Their use in the series is therefore limited.

A drilling machine will be required, but using the lathe for drilling as an alternative is briefly considered.

Whilst the use of cutting tools with replaceable tips considerably reduces the amount of grinding necessary to produce and sharpen lathe tools, some specials are bound to be required. An off hand grinder is therefore a necessity.

Chucks

Having dealt with the machines there is a number of accessories that are a must. It is easy to fall into the trap of considering that, due to its ease of use, a 3-jaw chuck is the one to acquire if funds will run to one chuck only, this is not so. Whilst a 3-jaw chuck, even if old and worn, will be accurate enough for most work there will be a significant number of instances where this is not so.

The beginner may not be aware that when material is placed into a 3-jaw chuck the work piece is unlikely to run true, perhaps a total indicator reading (TIR) of up to 0.1mm, more if measured some distance from the jaws. This can cause serious problems with concentricity when an item has to be removed and replaced, say to work from either end.

1. Normal (left) and Reverse (right) chuck Jaws.

Even a so-called precision chuck, with a price tag to go with the precision, will be unable to meet the most demanding requirements. A 4-jaw chuck with independent jaws is therefore a necessity as, being able to adjust each jaw individually, precise centring is possible. Of course where a 3-jaw chuck is adequate I will use one and this is evident in the photographs published. Where a reader has only a 4-jaw chuck this will be quite satisfactory. The only result being to slow down the operation a little due to the work necessary to get the part to run sufficiently true for the task in hand.

An essential accessory for the 3-jaw chuck are the reverse jaws that enable larger diameters to be held and are seen on the right of **Photo 1**. A new chuck will always be supplied with these but if you have obtained a second hand chuck,

maybe with a second hand lathe, they may well be missing. Unfortunately, spare jaws are not easily obtained and a replacement chuck may be the only option. One set of jaws will suffice for the 4-jaw chuck as its differing construction permits the single set of jaws to by used either way round.

Changing the jaws on the 3-jaw chuck is straightforward; open the chuck with the normal jaws fitted, and keep turning until the jaws can be removed. Now it will be found that both chuck and jaws are numbered 1, 2 and 3 and must be fitted with the numbers together and in that order. Turn the scroll in the direction to close the chuck, until its leading edge is seen to pass position 1. Next reverse the rotation until the leading edge passes back, fit jaw number 1 pushing it in as far as it will go. Then holding it there, again turn the chuck key as to tighten the chuck. Watch carefully

2. Fixed (on the left) and travelling steadies

for the scrolls leading edge to pass position 2, repeat the exercise and then also for jaw 3. Now close the chuck until the jaws meet in the middle. If you have made an error it will be large enough to be obvious and it will then be a case of repeat the task until all's well. Independent jaw 4- jaw chucks also have their jaws numbered and should be assembled with like numbers together, though they can of course be assembled in any order.

Having said that the reverse jaws are for larger diameters it is necessary to know at what diameter the change over must take place. If a new chuck is purchased the data supplied with it should make this clear; my 100mm chuck quotes a maximum of 33mm. Whilst the jaws will open and grip a larger diameter some of the scroll will be disengaging from the teeth on the jaws placing more load on those remaining

engaged. Frequently, scrolls will have just two rings, so if a scroll is not engaged only one ring and a single tooth are being used. It is not advisable therefore to go beyond the maker's recommendations. If these are not available careful observation of the scroll, which becomes visible as the chuck is opened, should make the requirements clear.

At this stage I should add that the book is written assuming a lathe of around 90mm bed to centre height and fitted with at least 100mm diameter chucks. Larger lathes are unlikely to impact on the book's content in any major way, though smaller lathes will and some comments are added through the series if considered appropriate. If a small lathe is being used then some items may benefit from being made smaller. In this case I would advise taking copies of the drawings and marking

3. Left (on the left) and Right hand Knife tools.

them up with the new dimensions in advance of making the item.

Steadies

Photo 2 shows both fixed (on the left) and travelling steadies. A fixed steady is, I consider, a very underestimated lathe accessory being an essential item, for without it many operations would be totally impossible, or at best very difficult. A fact that is well-illustrated thoughout the book. A travelling steady though is for most lathe users an item that has limited use and can be put on the end of the "items to be acquired list", though managing without it where a use for it exists can be a problem. Its use is illustrated in chapter 11 Photo 12.

Cutting tools

Various cutting tools will be required with the knife tool being that most used, and in both left and right handed versions. **Photo 3** shows some variations, I will refer to these throughout the book as, right hand on the right and left hand on the left. Right hand is used for cutting from right too left and Left hand from left to right. I make this precise definition as I find in the wider world there seems to be some variation in the meaning of left and right hand.

Also required are boring tools for a minimum bore of 6mm, say 20mm deep, and larger diameters of 20mm and more with a depth of say 50mm. Whilst knife tools can be ground from high speed steel, ready made brazed tungsten carbide tipped tools or replaceable tip tools are available as seen in the photograph and at a reasonable price. This is certainly not the case for very smaller boring tools which most certainly have to be ground from high speed steel tool bits, as whilst they are available their price probably

4. A rear tool post is almost essential for parting off on the smaller lathe.

prohibits their use in most home workshops. Some specialised tools will also be required, thread cutting, etc., and will be discussed at the point in the book where they become necessary.

Parting off tools and rear tool post

Parting off is probably the most dreaded of all turning operations for the small lathe user but is a task that must be conquered. Taking the part from the chuck and cutting it off with a hacksaw whilst held in the vice is a possibility and one that we shall adopt initially. Eventually though, parting off must be mastered and hopefully before the end of the book.

I know you will be tempted to cut off a part using the hacksaw whilst the part is still held in the lathe, we all are. I would not recommend this but if you do succumb to the temptation, do protect the lathe bed with a block of wood and move the saddle well down the lathe to avoid catching ones knuckles on the cutting tools. Even with this done, cover the tools with a few layers of substantial cloth and DO NOT UNDER ANY CIRCUMSTANCES carry out the operation with the lathe running.

We therefor need parting off tools of varying widths to use with differing diameters. It should be obvious that you would not use a 3mm wide tool to part off a part from a 4mm diameter bar and that a 0.5mm wide tool would be more appropriate. On the other hand a 0.5mm tool would not be at all appropriate at 50mm diameter and a wider tool would be required.

Whilst parting off tools can be used

mounted on the top slide the use of a rear tool post will significantly ease the task. Having one available cannot be too strongly advised particularly for larger diameters, **Photo 4** shows a typical example.

Dial test indicator (DTI)

A dial test indicator is required, as some projects will need precisely centring in the 4-jaw chuck to a level of accuracy that is difficult without one.

Smaller Items

Hard (dead) and Soft (live) centres will be necessary for turning between centres and driving dogs for these operations. When facing the end of a part supported by the tailstock centre, machining the end fully is impossible no matter what tool is used. This problem is overcome by the use of what is called a "half centre", in fact it is more a case of a five eight's centre as it is not cut away totally to the centre. The cut away permits the cutting tool to access the face right up to the drilled impression, (see SK 1 Chapter 2). A small half centre made from silver steel and held in the drill chuck avoids the expense of an additional centre and is perfectly adequate for finishing the end of a part otherwise turned between conventional centres. Why not make this a mini project before turning starts in earnest in the next chapter.

A drill chuck and a 25mm outside micrometer also fall into the essential category with a 25 to 50mm micrometer and a 150mm vernier being highly desirable. Other simple items will be required and we will attempt to make some of these as the work progresses. This is in some cases essential as they are not available commercially. An important lesson to learn here is that even if a task can be undertaken with the equipment to hand, it can often be carried out, more simply, more quickly, or more accurately, by the addition of some simple home made accessory. Examples of this certainly surface throughout the book, typically the collet holding fixture in Photos 12 to 15, Chapter 13.

Material

This is detailed with each individual project and in the case of mild steel will probably be sizes that are already available in the workshop, though some larger sizes will no doubt have to be purchased. I would strongly recommend that all mild steel should be a genuine, free cutting grade purchased to specification rather than relying on unknown materials that are to hand.

If as a beginner you have yet to build up a stock of materials, do ensure that materials you purchase are of a known grade, as one supplier's so called "free cutting mild steel" may be quite different from that from another. I would suggest steel to BS970 1983 ref. 230M07 is obtained, (very similar to the older specification BS970 1955 ref. EN1A that is still frequently referred to) and the ends marked, perhaps stamped FC, so that its grade is known when used in the future. For non-UK readers 230M07 is an international standard and is likely to be understood by your local supplier. Even more easily machined is a similar grade but with lead added this has the reference of 230M07Pb (EN1APb). The lead content makes it very much easier to machine but also unsuitable for welding; it is of course a little more expensive and not available in so many shapes and sizes.

I cannot stress to strongly the benefit of taking such an approach; advice that I give gained from bitter experience. Recently, I made a gear hobbing machine that had two very similar spindles but one having a slightly larger diameter. Having completed the one satisfactorily I found the finish being obtained with the second was very inferior. Using the same tools, but re-sharpened in view of the problem, trying differing tools, speeds and feeds was all to no avail. The only answer was that the material, being a different diameter, was of a different and inferior grade.

In-depth detail

With the book being especially, though not entirely, aimed at the beginner, descriptions and photographic evidence of methods used is more extensive than is the norm. Operations will in some cases prompt for greater precision than perhaps is necessary, purely to acquire the experience. Similarly, set-ups will err on the side of caution, both for safety and experience. A typical case being the use of a fixed steady where perhaps with greater, first hand experience this could be avoided. I would therefore say, please do work to the methods proposed. You can take your own approach in the future as knowledge of the operations and the ability of the machines you are using is gained over years of use.

The beginner to using a metal working lathe can be forgiven for considering that coming to terms with the turning process is as follows. Chose the correct cutting tool for the job, the correct speed and the correct rate of feed and with this done the skill has been conquered. As important as these are, they do have considerable tolerance as to their choice. In most cases the critical decisions are the methods to use, typically, whether to use the 3 jaw, 4 jaw, faceplate or turn between centres. Of even greater importance in many cases is the machining sequence. It can be very frustrating to have machined a part to a stage where it is found difficult to progress further, say due to difficulty in holding it for the remaining operations. An example of this would be the need to support a part with a fixed steady but not having left a suitable portion of the component where the steady can be applied.

Frequently the difficulty in machining a part will be due to the design and if this is someone else's there is less scope to overcome the problem, though some minor changes may be possible. If you are producing your own design, then manufacturing the item on the machines available should be an essential early consideration of the design process.

Metric dimension

Much has been written regarding the use of metric dimensions and this is not the place to expand still further on the subject. The book is though dimensioned almost exclusively in metric dimensions, only where a part is to marry with a genuine imperial dimension will the imperial value be given. Realising though that many readers will have imperially calibrated machines some guidance is necessary, especially as the articles are aimed at the novice.

The complications in working to metric dimensions on an imperial machine are very overstated; in fact it is quite easy. Replacing your machinery for metric calibrated ones is quite unnecessary, the answer being in HAVING metric measuring equipment, NOT converting the metric dimensions given to their imperial equivalents. As some items are dual calibrated such as rules, verniers, height gauges, we are left only with micrometers. Purchasing a 0-25mm micrometer and if possible a 25-50mm version also, is a very cheap way out of the problem if the following approach is taken.

When carrying out machining operations, few if any will attempt to arrive at the final size taking just one sizeable cut. The work will be carried out on the basis of, measure, large cut to get closer to size, measure, small cut to get very close, measure, final very small cut to arrive at size. With that approach the following will make working to metric dimensions on an imperial machine a very easy operation. Measure the part and determine how many millimetres have to be removed then set the depth of cut on the basis that 1mm equals 0.040 in. (40 thou.). This will of course introduce a small error but as the part is to be measured again and a further cut taken the error will be of no importance. When getting closer to the size required, work on the basis that 0.1mm equals 0.004 in. (4 thou.). Again this will introduce an error but now very small, but will also be eliminated by further measurement if greater precision is required. If the part requires greater precision then work on the basis that 0.01mm equals 0.0004 in. (0.4 thou.) As 0.01mm equals 0.0003937 in, this is an error of 0.0000063 in., which is quite insignificant even if you are taking a cut of many times this amount.

The point to realise is that the errors introduced by using these conversion factors get eliminated at each stage by the part being measured again in metric dimensions.

Approach to a project

Having first decided that an item is a project worth undertaking there are a number of preliminary actions that should be considered a must. First, and vitally important, is to study the drawings so that you fully understand what has to be made and in particular how the parts interrelate. In industry, part drawings would include tolerances so that parts made at separate times, and maybe in different locations, can be guaranteed to fit together when coming together for assembly. In the home workshop this is rarely necessary as the second part can be made to fit the first. If tolerances were quoted and a small error was made in the first part, few would be prepared to scrap this if a small adjustment to the size of the second would permit the first still to be used. Understanding the drawings is therefore an essential part of this approach. Next, as far as is practicable, determine the manufacturing methods. However, through this book I will be detailing these and would advise staying with them to gain the experience intended. For any projects undertaken beyond those in the book you will of course be "on you own".

Terms

TIR. Total indicator reading. When a part is running out of true an indicator applied to it will deflect positively on one side by the amount of the error. At 180 degrees from this position however the deflection will be negative, again by the error. The movement of the indicator is therefore called the "Total indicator reading" being twice the error present.

DTI. Dial test indicator. Strictly speaking this is a measuring instrument for measuring small differences in position. This usually has a small swinging arm for applying to the workpiece and its measuring range is in the order of +/- 1mm only. This compares with a "Dial Indicator" that normally has a plunger to apply to the workpiece and has a range of 10mm plus. Of course a Dial Indicator can be used in place of a Dial test indicator, and in home workshop terminology the two terms are often confused.

Chapter 2

Mini Surface Gauge

Having gone into so much general detail in the last Chapter, let us now get down to some project work. This initial project is a small surface gauge that will be ideal for the marking out of very small components. Whilst small, its main feature is a design that is unconventional. The reason for this is to provide sufficient basic turning to get the novice up and running, or should that be up and turning.

Base (5)

This requires the material to be reduced in diameter from 40mm to 12mm over a length of 55mm giving plenty of scope at this early stage to experiment with differing speeds, feeds and depth of cut. Whilst different tools could also be tried this would over complicate the issue, so carry out the operation with the preferred knife tool of your choice, (high speed steel, replaceable tip or brazed tungsten carbide). If you have a replaceable tip knife tool I would though suggest using this.

First, cut a 77mm length of 40mm diameter trying to keep the cut end as square as is possible. Place this in the 3-jaw (I will not continue to give this alternative but of course the 4-jaw if this is

all you have) and immediately it is likely to be found that the diameter is too large for the chuck's normal jaws. If so, fit the reverse jaws as described in Chapter 1.

When attempting to hold the material with the reverse jaws, another very important fact becomes obvious. That is, the length of grip will be much less than with the normal jaws, typically in the order of 8mm. The result is to limit the length of the material that can be safely held without additional support. As a guide, no more projecting than the material diameter, rather less at larger diameters. An exception to this rule is where the part has only to be centre drilled and possibly drilled. In this case the end only load will ensure that the part is not forced from the chucks jaws, as would be the case with a side load.

As the part has sawn ends they are likely to be out of square with the axis. The effect of this is that if the end is held firmly against the jaw treads (for want of another description I am using the stairway terms of treads and risers) whilst the chuck is tightened, then the outer end of the bar will not run true. This is due to the limited length of grip of the riser having minimal effect in pulling the bar into line. Therefore, tighten

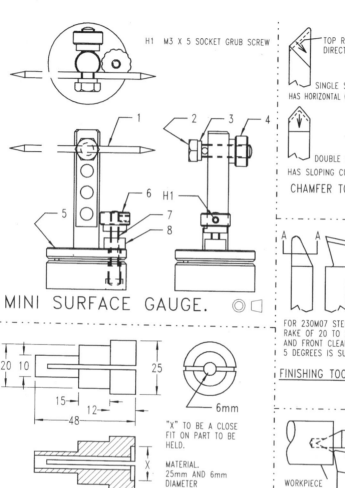

H1 M3 X 5 SOCKET GRUB SCREW

1
2   3   4
5
6 H1
7
8

MINI SURFACE GAUGE. ◎◁

20 10
15
12
48
25
6mm

"X" TO BE A CLOSE FIT ON PART TO BE HELD.

MATERIAL.
25mm AND 6mm DIAMETER 230M07 STEEL

◎◁

2
20   6

REMACHINING PLUG

THIN PIECE COLLET.   SK 4.

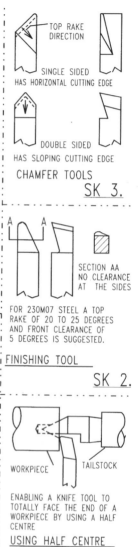

TOP RAKE DIRECTION

SINGLE SIDED
HAS HORIZONTAL CUTTING EDGE

DOUBLE SIDED
HAS SLOPING CUTTING EDGE

CHAMFER TOOLS
SK 3.

A   A

SECTION AA
NO CLEARANCE
AT THE SIDES

FOR 230M07 STEEL A TOP RAKE OF 20 TO 25 DEGREES AND FRONT CLEARANCE OF 5 DEGREES IS SUGGESTED.

FINISHING TOOL
SK 2.

WORKPIECE   TAILSTOCK

ENABLING A KNIFE TOOL TO TOTALLY FACE THE END OF A WORKPIECE BY USING A HALF CENTRE

USING HALF CENTRE
SK 1.

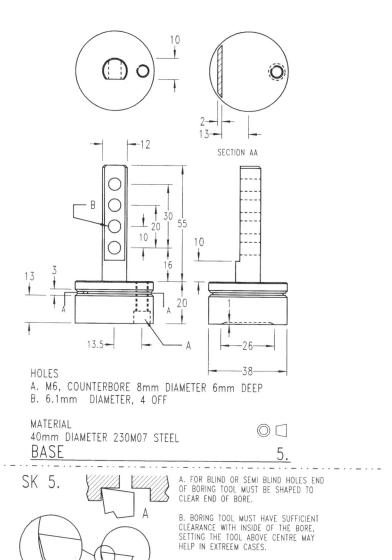

SECTION AA

HOLES
A. M6, COUNTERBORE 8mm DIAMETER 6mm DEEP
B. 6.1mm   DIAMETER, 4 OFF

MATERIAL
40mm DIAMETER 230M07 STEEL

BASE   5.

SK 5.

A. FOR BLIND OR SEMI BLIND HOLES END
OF BORING TOOL MUST BE SHAPED TO
CLEAR END OF BORE.

B. BORING TOOL MUST HAVE SUFFICIENT
CLEARANCE WITH INSIDE OF THE BORE,
SETTING THE TOOL ABOVE CENTRE MAY
HELP IN EXTREEM CASES.

BORING TOOL FORM

1. *Advancing the cross slide slowly, and with a small piece of wood in the tool holder, eases the workpiece to run true as the lathe is TURNED BY HAND. The chuck is initially only lightly tightened*

the chuck only just enough to grip the part without falling out, rotate the chuck by hand and ease the outer end until it is running reasonably true. The best way to carrying out this operation is with a blunt object mounted on the top slide as follows. The cross slide is advanced very slowly as the part is rotated by hand until the part is running true, when the chuck can then be fully tightened, checking that the part still runs true. A white piece of card behind the gap will aid visibility, as it will in other cases where a small gap is being observed. UNDER NO CIRCUMSTANCES, attempt this process with the lathe running, even slowly. **Photo 1** shows this having been done though the photograph was taken after the end had also been centre drilled.

The part is now ready for centre drilling in preparation for supporting with the tailstock centre. Do this with the part running at about 1000rpm and using a small centre drill, drilling to 5mm diameter. I would not recommend much greater projection than this, even for this task. It is possible if the part is running a little off centre, for the out of balance forces exerted, to throw the part from the chuck as it runs up to speed, extreme caution is therefore very much the approach to take. Of course, running the lathe at a rather slow speed for the operation will help to avoid any problem.

Which Centre?

In Chapter 1, hard and soft centres were indicated as a necessity but you may have

2. When working with this length of workpiece, the outer end must be supported; in this case with the tailstock centre, in some cases though with a fixed steady.

wondered why one hard and one soft. When using a centre in the tailstock this is termed a dead centre as it does not rotate with the workpiece and as a result needs to be hardened so as to withstand the wear this creates. You may ask therefore why not for simplicity obtain two hardened centres, be patient; the reason for this should become apparent in Chapter 4.

The task is now to face the outer end of the part whilst supported with the tailstock centre, making sure it is the hard centre that is fitted. With a drop of oil on the centres tip, advance it until resistance is felt and then lock the barrel of the tailstock. For most turning using the tailstock centre, it is necessary to reset the tailstock occasionally as the heat generated

expands the work piece. With so little machining necessary at this stage this will not occur but some bedding in of the centre may result in a need for some initial readjustment.

Using the chosen knife tool, face the end as close to the centre as is possible, but, unless you have a half centre (SK 1) it will not be possible to get fully to the centre drilled impression, this though is not a problem in this case. **Photo 2** shows the operation. Whilst it has been said that any form of knife tool can be used there are subtle differences that have to be taken note of. For want of a better term, the "conventional knife tool" has a top rake that limits its use to cutting on its left edge, that is when fed right to left. A variation on this

3. There is plenty of material to remove giving plenty of opportunity to experiment with speed, depth of cut and feed rate.

is its use for facing, where the cutting edge must be set at a slight angle with the tip closer to the chuck. With the tool set like this, start at the centre of the work piece, place a depth of cut (right to left) of say 0.05mm, and face the end by winding the cross slide towards you, in this way the tool will cut on its intended cutting edge. There are though few hard and fast rules in this activity and if the tool was fed in the reverse direction it would cut, though almost certainly producing an inferior finish.

If using a replaceable tip cutter this will have a top rake that permits it to cut on all its sides and the radiused corners also. With this tool therefore it will quite adequately cut whilst being fed in and cuts of 0.5mm wide are quite feasible. It is the case that many of the methods used in the past with conventional tools of the day are

not fully appropriate with the more adaptable form of cutting edge found on replaceable tipped tools.

With the part's first end now surfaced, albeit not fully to the centre, it can be removed and fitted the other way round. With the end now surfaced and at right angles to the part's axis, the end can be held against the jaw treads prior to tightening, the unfinished centre portion of the end should sit between the open end of the jaws. This time the work piece should run adequately true without further adjustment and can again be centre drilled for supporting with the tailstock centre. As some lengthy turning operations are to be undertaken, this time centre drill to 8mm so as to give a larger bearing surface.

Again support the work with the centre, lubricate and adjust as already advised.

4. Using a tool with a radiused end and a honed edge will result in a good finish.

However, this time, with a lot of metal to be removed its temperature will rise causing it to expand, increasing the pressure of the centre in the centred end. It will be necessary therefore to release the centre and readjust it periodically (not while a cut is being taken).

With the part chucked and supported, a start can be made to reduce the outer diameter to 12mm over a length to give a base depth of 21mm. Experiment with differing speeds, depths of cut and rates of feed during the process. With the machine running at 300rpm, or thereabouts, take a first cut of 1mm depth, hand feed it at a rate that you feel at home with. Hand feed for experience even if your lathe is equipped with automatic fine feed. There are no hard and fast rules regarding speeds, feeds and depth of cut. What

works, works, but so do many other combinations. Follow this with cuts of 1.5mm and 2mm deep, if your lathe is sound, then more than 2mm should be possible but stick to this maximum at this point, see **Photo 3**.

Continue reducing the diameter but, whilst speeds are not as critical as some lists would have one believe, 300rpm will become on the slow side as the diameter reduces. Theoretically, the attempt is to keep the surface speed the same for the smaller diameters, so at half the diameter double the speed. Therefore, at about 20mm diameter increase the speed to 600 rpmand approaching 12mm to 1000rpm. If for any reason, you feel these speeds are high, run the lathe slower but still increase the speed proportionately (approximately) as the diameter reduces.

When the diameter reaches 12.3mm change tools for the finishing tool seen in SK 2 and **Photo 4**. This is used to take cuts of no more than 0.05mm and, as seen in a Chapter 5, Photo 1, can take very fine cuts if honed to a fine edge. The significant aspect of this tool is that whilst it feeds right to left, (or left to right) as does a knife tool, the top rake is back to front. Other writers will suggest other tools to acquire a good finish but in any case, its use when finishing to a very precise diameter, this tool takes some beating.

Producing the "finishing tool"

Shaping the tool is simple, as there are no clearance angles on either side, only on the front edge and front to back rake on the top. **Photo 5** shows the front edge being finished on the side of the wheel (use the side of the wheel for light grinding only). Unfortunately, no "run of the mill" off hand grinder comes with adequate work tables, most are very inadequate. Because of this, a better table such as that in the photograph should be a must. Finally finish the cutting edge with a fine carborundum stone.

Back to the base

With the 12mm diameter finished, return the knife tool and very lightly face the top of the base leaving it still a little over 20mm. To do this move the tip of the tool so that it just touches the 12mm diameter and feeding it to the left to produce a cut of about 0.05mm depth, facing the surface by slowly winding the tool out. Repeat the process as necessary to achieve a fully machined face and a 20mm + dimension. Next stage is to face the top of the upright to bring it to a length of 55mm. Removing the centre and machining the end

5. Shaping the end of the tool seen in Photo 4. An adjustable tool rest such as this will give much better results than unaided free hand grinding and should be considered an essential part of the workshop equipment.

unsupported is an option but the sawn end, even at that small diameter, may give an intermittent cut so caution is being advised. Because of this the fixed steady is being used to support the part. Disengage the centre and fit the steady in a position, some

6. A fixed steady is an essential accessory for serious lathe work.

7. Recessing the underneath of the base using a standard knife tool. If the tool rubs rather than cuts try a shallower angle or set the tool above centre height.

20mm from the end, reapply the centre and set the steady arms to touch the upright. This is an undemanding application for the steady and more will be said about its use in future projects. With the steady set, remove the centre and face the end of the upright to arrive at 55mm. With the steady still in place also chamfer the top of the upright as shown in **Photo 6**. This shows a single sided chamfer tool (SK 3) ground from high speed steel, though if you have a range of replaceable tipped tools you may have one that will suit the operation, though not giving a 45 degree chamfer unless the tool is set at an angle. In some cases this may result in the tool fouling with the chuck and much care must be taken. The dedicated chamfer tool is therefore to be preferred and is a good early exercise in shaping your own high speed steel tools.

You could rather than making left and right hand forms make the universal tool also shown in SK 3.

The base can now be removed from the chuck and reversed for machining the underside and outer diameter, but the normal jaws will have to be returned. Having paid so much attention to giving the upright a good finish it would be a pity to mark this by clamping it in the chuck without some protection. Bend a piece of thin copper around the upright taking care to see that it does not overlap, place in the chuck with the top of the base resting against the jaws, tighten and face the underside to give the 20mm dimension.

The gauge when finished will sit more precisely on the surface plate if the base is recessed in the centre. Do this by setting the knife tool round to about 30 degrees and starting from the centre, wind the tool out taking cuts of about 0.2mm depth, stopping some 6mm short of the edge, as seen in **Photo 7**. Repeat until the recess is 1mm deep and 26mm diameter. If the tool tends to rub, set the angle shallower and place on lighter cuts, setting the tool above centre will also help. More will be discussed about tool height setting throughout the chapters.

Next turn the outer diameter to 38mm checking this with a micrometer, vernier or use some good old-fashioned callipers and a rule. Do remember to reduce the speed now machining is again at a larger diameter. Accuracy of the outside diameter and its finish is of no importance other than that achieving it is good experience for future projects.

Method of adjustment

The method of adjustment is, to say the least, unconventional, but with the gauge finished it is tried and tested and I can confirm it works. It only gives though the final small adjustment, say plus and minus 0.5mm.

A slot is cut in the base leaving a web, the elasticity of which provides the flexibility required. The drawing for the base (5) shows this clearly in the section AA view and quotes a thickness of 2mm. This is for guidance only as the width should be reduced in stages until sufficient flexibility is provided and the adjustment can be achieved with relative ease.

For most, the only way of creating the slot will be to saw it using a hand held hack saw and whilst this should be no problem it is likely to be visually poor. A way of overcoming this is to turn a groove first so that the edge produced is regular. This can

8. Using a left hand knife tool, and with the top slide set to 45 degrees, to produce a 'V' groove.

then be used as a guide for sawing and will camouflage the wavy edge produced by the saw. A "V" form slot is produced for this purpose using a left hand knife tool and with the top slide set to 45 degrees and making the grove as illustrate in **Photo 8**. Now make the chamfer on the top side of the base using the same set up. Access to the edge should be easy but do take care making sure the tool does not foul the chuck in any way, turn the chuck by hand prior to running it under power.

HOLES
A. M6

MATERIAL
15mm DIAMETER 230M07 STEEL

SCRIBER NUT.   4.

HOLES
A. M4
B. M3

MATERIAL
15mm DIAMETER 230M07 STEEL

ADJUSTER NUT   6.

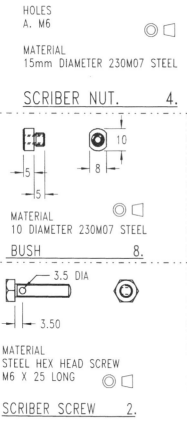

MATERIAL
10 DIAMETER 230M07 STEEL

BUSH   8.

MATERIAL
STEEL HEX HEAD SCREW
M6 X 25 LONG

SCRIBER SCREW   2.

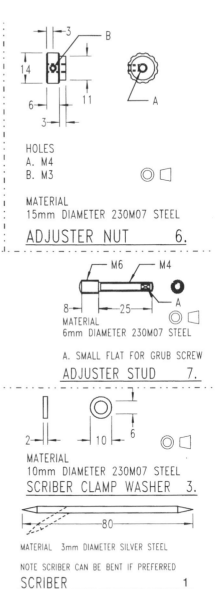

MATERIAL
6mm DIAMETER 230M07 STEEL

A. SMALL FLAT FOR GRUB SCREW

ADJUSTER STUD   7.

MATERIAL
10mm DIAMETER 230M07 STEEL

SCRIBER CLAMP WASHER   3.

MATERIAL   3mm DIAMETER SILVER STEEL

NOTE SCRIBER CAN BE BENT IF PREFERRED

SCRIBER   1

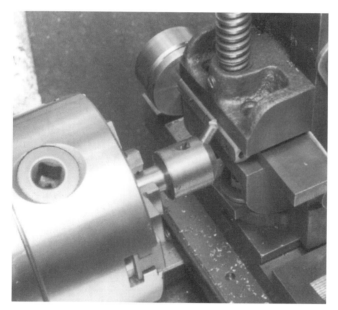

9. Even if you have a milling machine using the lathe is still worthwhile in some cases. Using a fly cutter to produce the flat on the base upright.

Fly cutting

There are still some holes required and a flat that we will now create on the lathe using a fly cutter as seen in **Photo 9**. Even if you own a milling machine it is still worth considering using the lathe for simple tasks as some jobs may be easier to set up on the lathe and a few, much easier.

If you have a drilling machine, and I assume most will, the most logical way to make the holes would be to use this. However, for those who do not I am illustrating in **Photo 10** how the four holes in the upright can be drilled using a lathe. Little explanation is required but rather than marking out the holes and then centre punching, their positions were established using the lathes leadscrew dials. The holes were initially started with a centre drill, actually easier than marking out and drilling. With the same drill pad, but rotated through 90 degrees, the hole in the base for the adjustment screw can be drilled and counterbored, see **Photo. 11**. Choose a drill to give around 65% thread depth (5.2mm for M6) as this will make taping the hole an easy operation minimising the possibility of tap breakage. Hand tap the hole completely through from below. An alternative form of drill pad to that mounted on the lathe's top slide is an adapter for mounting the lathe's faceplate on the tailstock. This results in what one may call a horizontal drilling machine.

The scriber assembly

Screw (2). The screw is a standard M6 x 25 Hexagon head screw with just a single hole drilled into it. For appearance sake the top surface of the head can be faced and re-chamfered and the end of the thread similarly improved.

10. If you do not yet have a drilling machine all is not lost. With a drill pad on the top slide the four holes in the column are drilled. The top slide is set at an angle to miss the tailstock, feed being applied by the leadscrew.

11. With the drill pad turned through 90 degrees the hole in the base can similarly be drilled.

12. *The gauge being put to use. Note the method of finishing the outer diameters of the adjusting screws.*

Scriber (1). The scriber is made from 3mm silver steel with the pointed end made on the grinding machine. To harden, just hold the tip in the flame until the end 3mm becomes red hot, the colour of boiled carrots viewed in good but not bright light. Hold in the flame for a few seconds to retain colour and then quench in water. Having hardened just the tip there should be no need to temper the part, hone the end to a good sharp point.

Scriber nut (4). This nut would normally have a knurled head, but as this task has not yet been discussed an alternative is suggested. Having made it this way you may even find you prefer it, I did. With the material in a 3-jaw chuck turn the smaller diameter, plunge the parting off tool about 3mm and at just over the width of the head. Centre drill, drill and tap M6. Tapping is done manually, not under power.

Now, with any tool on the top slide that will scribe a line, proceed as follows. Place one of the three jaws horizontal at the front and by traversing the saddle, scribe a line using the tool you have fitted. Bring the next jaw to the horizontal and repeat, similarly for the third jaw. Repeat the process with the three jaws horizontal at the rear, vertically above and vertically below, resulting in 12 scribed lines. Follow this by parting off at just over length.

With the part held in a vice and using a small round file, about 3 to 4mm diameter, file a grove in the head at each scribed line, making each grove about 2mm wide. This can be seen in **Photo 12** that shows the finished surface gauge being used. Return the part to the chuck holding it on the reduced diameter and skim over the outer diameter to clean up the filed edges, face and chamfer the outer end. Grip a length of M6 studding in the chuck and fit the nut the other way round enabling the other edge of the head to be chamfered also.

Scriber clamp washer (3)

Place a piece of 10mm steel in the chuck, face the end, centre drill, drill and part off at about 2.5mm thick. The ultimate thickness of the washer is quite critical so as to ensure that it is the washer that clamps the scriber and not the inside of the hole on the clamping screw. This has been established to create a deliberate need to work on thin parts. You may feel what is being proposed is rather over involved, and this may be the case. Although the small collet has to be made, it is used a number of times throughout the book, so do not be tempted to bypass the operation. You will eventually need it for operations where there is very little alternative.

Thin Piece Collet (SK 4)

The answer to the problems of working on thin pieces is to use a thin piece collet and whilst these can be a sizeable project to make, a simple alternative is possible where concentricity is not over important. The collet suggested is intended to be held in the 3 or 4-jaw chuck so no other item is required, other than the plug that makes it possible to machine the end for use with other diameters, larger or smaller. After its initial use has expired, the end can be subsequently opened up for larger

13. Boring the thin piece collet prior to being slotted and used for machining a washer.

diameters, or the head reduced in length and bored for smaller diameters. In the first instance the collet will be bored prior to it being slotted, **Photo. 13**. Subsequently, this will not be the case and the plug will be fitted to prevent the collet closing whilst held for re-boring.

Boring, covered more fully in Chapter 7, is much more complex than outside diameter turning, especially at smaller diameters. Shaping the tool is all-important to gain the clearance between it and bore being made as shown in SK 5. Take note that the shape of boring tool in SK 5 not only permits the tool to move right to left for boring, but also away from the operator

14. *Using the thin piece collet to hold a washer whilst being machined to the thickness required.*

using the cross slide enabling facing the base of the bore to be carried out. Having bored the end of the collet to be close fit on the washer it can be slotted using a hack saw. Remove any burs especially those in the bore and return the collet to the chuck and grip the washer ensuring it is properly located on the base of the bore and that the rear of the collet head is located against the chuck's jaws, **Photo 14**.

Place the scriber through the hole in the screw and using feeler gauges determine the distance between the scriber and the inside of the head. Lock the saddle and using the top slide to place a light cut face the washer using the cross slide. Do not move the top slide but remove the washer and measure its thickness. From

this you will be able to determine the amount still to be removed. It is now that one advantage of the collet surfaces, that is the part can be returned to exactly the same position enabling a known depth of cut to be easily established. It is of course essential that both washer and head of the collet be properly seated. When complete the washer should just slide in between the scriber and the head of the screw, thus ensuring that the washer and not the screw grips the scriber.

Adjuster assembly

Adjuster nut (6) This is virtually a repeat of item 4, the through hole is though M4 and it has the addition of hole B (M3)

Adjuster Stud (7) Chuck a piece of 6mm steel set the speed to around 2000rpm and turn down to 4mm over 25mm length. If your lathe does not run at so high a speed, and many do not, use the highest speed available. Using threading dies on the lathe is covered in Chapter 7 as is making holders for them. Without such facility, remove to the vice and make the threads using a hand held diestock. Concentricity of the threads is though of importance and making them a little on the slack side will help, the reason for this becoming obvious when assembling the parts is covered. Once tailstock die holders are available you may like to remake this part.

Bush (8) Chuck a length of 10mm diameter drill and tap M4, turn down the end to 6mm diameter and thread M6 and part off. Return to the chuck very carefully holding it on the M6 thread, it will not eventually be seen so any small mark on the thread will be of no consequence, face and chamfer the end. If you wish you can mill the flats, but for such a small operation improve your hand work skills and file them.

Assembly

With all the parts now having been completed there remains only their assembly. This is a little more complex than probably you anticipate. The scriber assembly is straightforward and needs no explanation, but this is not so for the adjuster mechanism. Study the assembly drawing and the individual parts and you will become aware that the difference between the pitch of the M6 thread and the M4 thread are being used to control the gap between top and bottom halves of the base, as created by the saw cut. With M6 having a pitch of 1mm and M4 a pitch of 0.7mm the resulting differential being a pitch of 0.3mm. Not only does this make turning the screw to affect an adjustment easier, of greater importance is that it can also jack open the slot as well as closing it, thereby increasing the adjustment range.

One feature of the mechanism is that as the gap is opened and closed the axis of two inside threads become miss-aligned and this probably limits the range over which adjustment can be achieved. Making the threads on the adjuster stud (7) on the small side, as suggested above, limits the effect of the miss-aligned axis.

To assemble, run the bush down the adjuster stud leaving some 3mm gap between the bush and the M6 threaded portion, also run down an M4 locking nut. Now using an M6 screw as a gauge, check that the two M6 threads are on the same pitch. If for example you find an error of half a pitch it would be easy to fall into the trap of thinking that you had to turn the bush just half a turn. This is not so as the differential effect will make it necessary to turn the bush by much more, this can result in the M6 portion on the stud and the bush itself being further apart than expected. As it is impossible to control the relative positions of the two threads on the stud and similarly those on the bush it is similarly impossible to control how this assembly turns out.

Having aligned the two M6 threads lock them in this position using the lock nut fitted and screw them as a pair into the base using an 8mm spanner to lock the bush in place. Remove the lock nut and fit the adjuster nut securing this with an M3 grub screw. At this point attempt to adjust the gauge but if as dimensioned you left the web at 2mm thick it will probably be hard to turn. Using the hack saw on the accessible side of the web, gradually reduce the thickness until adjustment becomes easy. Do take note though that as the gap is opened, or closed, the threads become miss aligned and so become stiff to operate, this is really beyond the intended range for the adjustment, so do not continue to thin the web or else you may end up with two pieces.

Final comment

With the gauge now complete and ready for use I do hope that you will find it useful, as you will see I have made use of it for marking out items later in the book. In the next chapter we will be dealing with an item that is outwardly much more simple. Of greater importance is that as a result of making the item future turning operations will be much more satisfying, we are talking about setting up the lathe to turn parallel. This is much more crucial than is often portrayed as there is no point in making a part within say +/- 0.002mm if over the length of the part there is an out of parallel amount of 0.01mm. If you own a lathe that you know does not turn parts parallel and you cannot see any adjustment to overcome this do not give up, you will be pleased to know there is almost certainly something that can be done to correct this and it is not complex. All is revealed in the next chapter.

Terms

Top Rake. This is the angle from the horizontal of the top face of a lathe tool. This varies according to material being turned but for the use tools get in the home workshop the value is not that critical.

Typically anywhere between 15 and 25 degrees when used with free cutting mild steel. The cutting tip is invariably higher and the rake slopes down from this, in a few cases the cutting tip is at the lowest point and the rake is called negative, some plastic materials prefer a negative rake of a few degrees. Some grades of brass use tools with zero rake.

Right hand tool. For this book, one that has its cutting edge on the left and cuts from right to left. In the wider world this definition is not consistent as some types of tool (mostly brazed tipped tools) refer to a tool with its cutting edge on the right.

Left hand tool. Visa Versa

Chapter 3

Precision Square

"Turning Parallel" (A MUST!)

This project is outwardly the most simple in the book but with an importance equal to any of them. Surprisingly, it is a single turned part with outside diameter and length not at all important and yet it is potentially the most accurate item that will be made. We are talking about angular accuracy and the item being a cylindrical square. The essential feature is that its outside diameter must be very accurately parallel along its length and is the reason for its inclusion here.

It is understandable that a beginner may consider a well-made lathe will automatically produce a parallel result. This is not so, and if the error is sufficient, satisfactory work will be difficult to achieve. He or she may also think that if such an error exists, the lathe is at fault and there is little that can rectify it, for most lathe's this is not so.

First, it must be realised that no piece of metal is totally rigid and a typical cast lathe bed is no exception. A major consideration is the effect of mounting the lathe onto an uneven surface distorting the lathe's bed in so doing. However, this cause of a problem can also be used to advantage, with packing placed under the lathe's feet any inherent error can be minimised. The approach of a jacking screw under each mounting **(Photo 1)** rather than packing is to be preferred. By this method very small adjustments can be made with ease to overcome errors created by the mounting or inherent in the lathe itself.

Mounting Requirements

There is an essential requirement for any method of adjustment adopted, and that is that the mounting must be sufficiently strong to create the necessary forces to flex the lathe's bed. Of course, the force

1. *A jacking screw under the lathe foot makes adjustment of the lathe relatively easy.*

required will both bend the lathe's bed and the mounting surface itself, and for it to work adequately the mounting must have a strength comparable to that of the lathe. It must therefore be mounted on a very rigid frame, ideally of welded construction. Even so the frame can be used with a wooden bench top, positioned above or below this.

If you have read other articles you may have come to the conclusion that the lathe must be mounted with its bed level to a very high degree of accuracy, as frequently a precision level is deemed necessary. This is not so and some articles do qualify this point. What is in fact necessary is that there is no twist along the length of the bed, and the only easy way to check this is by using a precision level so that if both ends are level then the lathe's bed is not twisted. It would also be free of any twist if the bed sloped by 1.000 degree at each end, but

how do you reliably measure such a deviation?

Unfortunately, precision levels are expensive, but all is not lost if a level is not to hand, as has been said it is not necessary that the bed is exactly level. Having mounted and adjusted the lathe (both across and along the bed) using a basic spirit level a test piece can be turned and measured and from the result the direction of adjustment can be determined. After adjustment, the test piece is again turned over its length and once more measured. Further adjustments can then be made and the process repeated until a virtually, error free parallel result is attained.

Before this test is carried out it is essential that the lathe is correctly adjusted in other respects. The spindle's bearings must be adjusted to be easy running but free of any clearance and similarly the

2. Turning a test piece for checking if the lathe turns parallel. Despite the length of the part it has to be turned unsupported, light cuts are therefore essential.

various slides must be set up for relatively easy movement but again free of any clearance that could result in errors being produced.

For the checks to be effective the test piece must be sufficiently long to ensure that any error can be detected. Twenty-five millimetre diameter with around 100mm projecting from the chuck holding it will be about right. The 25mm will ensure that bending, as a result of the cut being taken will be negligible.

Having turned the bar and taken the first set of measurements some adjustment will almost certainly be necessary. Typically, if the test piece is larger at the outer end, then the front mounting at the tailstock end requires to be raised, or if smaller, then the mounting requires to be lowered. The adjustment can of course be made at any foot providing the effect is to twist the bed

in the appropriate direction. Even if the lathe is set up using a precision level, a test piece should still be turned and minor adjustments carried out. With repeated machining and checking, one should be aiming at a virtually error free result, certainly no more than 0.002mm on diameter over the 100mm length.

You may question the machining of a part projecting so far from the chuck, without its outer end supported, typically the tailstock centre, if so, one is correct to question such an operation. However, if the tailstock is not exactly on the lathe's axis this would affect the end result, and would be at odds with the test's purposes. The effect of the tailstock will though be discussed in Chapter 4.

The statements so far assumes the use of a 100mm chuck such that the test piece, around 130mm total length, can be

3. The mini precision cylindrical square alongside a normal square.

held over a length of at least 20mm using the standard jaws, as in **Photo 2**. If a smaller chuck is being used, probably on a smaller lathe, then the size will need to be scaled down appropriately.

An Alternative

There are other possible methods, one consists of taking a bar, say 300mm long by 25mm diameter and mounting this in the 4-jaw, setting it to run true at the jaws, testing this with a dial test indicator. Without moving anything, other than running the saddle to the outer end of the bar, rotate the lathe BY HAND and take note of the dial test indicator readings. From these determine the mean value, that is midway between the maximum and minimum readings (it is unlikely that the outer end will be running true). By adjusting the lathe's mounting, the aim is to get the mean reading at the outer end the same as that

at the chuck's jaws. Do take note though, that having made adjustments it will be necessary to check the dial test indicator reading at both the chuck and the outer end of the bar. An advantage of this system is that the test piece can be much longer as no machining takes place, there is though no feeling of certainty as there is if a test piece is turned and measured for the purpose. Perhaps is should be used as a first stage, followed by turning a test piece.

Cylindrical Square

With the lathe now turning parallel it is time to make the Cylindrical Square, **Photo 3**, as a final test of your efforts. If you think it is a bit of a gimmick, then it is worth noting that one 150mm high and 100mm diameter is likely to set you back some £100+, it is of course hardened and ground to a very high standard of accuracy. Its use is as a reference for inspection work on precision

4. Recessing the base of the square with the part supported by a home -made half centre mounted in the drill chuck.

components. In the home workshop cruder versions can be used for a number of purposes but more about that later.

Mount in the 3 jaw chuck a length of 25mm diameter steel, about 90mm long, and with 65mm projecting, centre drilling the end ready for supporting with the tailstock centre. With this done, face the end, and recess it with the tool set at an angle (see Photo.7 Chapter 2 as an example). Do this as close to the tailstock centre as is possible, though as will be seen later it is not that critical. I used a home made half centre in the drill chuck, as shown in **Photo 4**, enabling facing to be achieved completely to the drilled centre. A speed of around 600rpm is suggested, though as commented on previously speeds are very much dependent on circumstances, material, tool being used, rigidity of machine, so continue experimenting.

Now turn the outside to 24mm diameter

using a knife tool, if you are not using a replaceable tip tool that will have a radiused tip ensure your conventional knife tool has a small flat on the end, so as to obtain a fine finish. SK 1 illustrates this type of tool, the flat having a similar effect to that of the finishing tool seen being used in **Photo 2**. Turning the outside diameter will have to be done without the tailstock centre engaged, so take light cuts only, 0.2mm initially, finally 0.05mm. Measure the part along its length using a micrometer and if parallel continue reducing the diameter until it measures 24mm. Whilst the diameter is not that important , an attempt to get very close will be useful experience.

However, if an error is found to exist resulting in the part not being parallel, it is a case of back to the original test piece, more light cuts and further adjustments. Returning the square to the 3-jaw it will again be necessary to true up the part

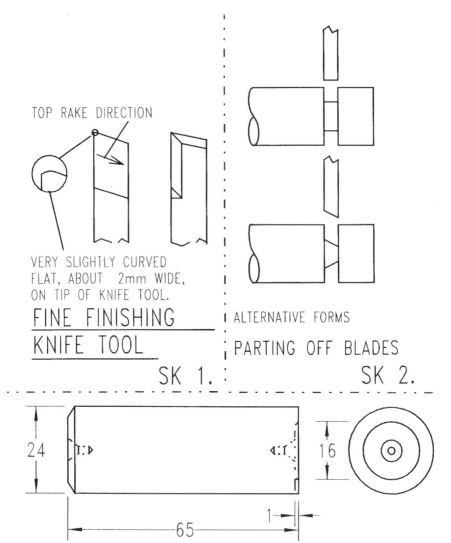

TOP RAKE DIRECTION

VERY SLIGHTLY CURVED
FLAT, ABOUT 2mm WIDE,
ON TIP OF KNIFE TOOL.

FINE FINISHING
KNIFE TOOL
SK 1.

ALTERNATIVE FORMS

PARTING OFF BLADES
SK 2.

24

1:▶   ◀:1

16

65   1

MATERIAL. 25mm DIAMETER 230M07 STEEL
PRECISION SQUARE.

followed by taking finishing cuts once more. If the part is now smaller than 24mm, as was said earlier, this is of no importance.

With the outer diameter parallel, now very lightly (0.02mm cuts) face just the outer ring of the end. This is absolutely essential, as only by turning the outer diameter and the end in succession can the accuracy of the base relative to the sides be ensured.

Parting off

Now comes the big test, parting off. Very much has been written regarding the process but one fact above all others that gets universal agreement, is that a rear tool post aids parting off considerably. It is therefore virtually essential on the average home workshop lathe. A fact that is less universally agreed on is the shape of the cutter. This can either be square or at a slight angle at the end, best understood by reference to SK2 (angle shown exaggerated, around 5 degrees would be normal). The principle of the angled end is that it frees the part being parted off without any projection on the end whilst the square ended tool may leave a small projection if it breaks at the material in the chuck first. The angled end is frequently used in production work as it can avoid the need for a further operation on the part being parted off.

The advantages of the square end are suggested as, 1. The angled end tends to cause the narrow blade to flex sideways creating a concave end and, 2. The angled tip produces swarf that is wider than the slot, making it more likely that the swarf will seize up in the slot being cut.
As with all turning tools the effect of them being mounted above centre height, (top slide mounted tools) is less crucial at larger diameters and heavier cuts. (See Chapter 5 SK1) With the parting off tool this can be a source of confusion for a tool that starts cutting well can refuse to cut as the diameter decreases. Do therefor ensure the cutting edge is a little low, say 0.1mm. (high in the case of a rear mounted tool).

Another good idea for larger diameters, is when the parting off operation is partially complete, is to wind the tool out, move it over say 0.4mm, and cut down the side of the already cut groove, return the tool to its original position and start parting off again. This wider slot will assist the swarf to fall away more freely.

We will now start the parting off operation. The length of the part and that of material quoted will mean that the tool will only be some 5mm from the chuck, do therefore before starting up the lathe, turn the lathe by hand to ensure that chuck and tool do not collide in any way. The closeness of cutter and chuck is though not a coincidence, as parting off should, unless the part is additionally supported by a steady or tailstock centre, always be carried out close to the chuck.

For a diameter of 24mm a speed of 600rpm has been suggested previously. However, for parting off I would initially say that a slightly lower speed is always a good idea, say 400 to 500rpm. Even so, as the diameter reduces, higher speeds should preferably be set up, say at 12mm, 1000rpm.

When carrying out the parting off operation do keep the tool feeding, probably more rapidly than you think correct. For some reason problems often materialise if the feed is slackened off or stopped altogether. Because of this, do wind the tool

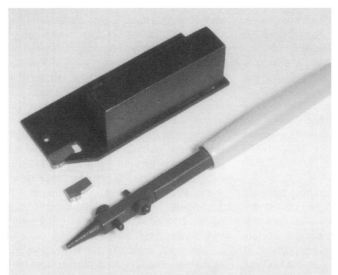

5. A parting off tool fitted with a replaceable tip. The photo also shows the tool supplied for removing and replacing tips.

out slightly any time you find it necessary to stop feeding it. Probably the most difficult aspect of parting off for the beginner is the effect of too slow a feed rate that can start the machine and workpiece vibrating. The understandable response is to reduce the feed rate still further. This though is likely to be the wrong response as an increase is more likely to prevent the vibration from getting out of control. I can only assume that the additional load of a greater feed rate stiffens up the machine in some way.

Developments in replaceable tip tooling means that even parting off tools can now be had with replaceable tips. Having obtained that in **Photo 5**, I can report that the results I am achieving with this are very encouraging and well worth the money spent.

Finishing the part

With the part now removed it can be finished off as follows. The part needs to be returned to the 3 jaw chuck, protecting the part from damage from the chuck's jaws by the use of thin copper sheet. Incidentally, a good source of copper for this is to take a short length of copper piping and slit it down its length on one side, then open it up and flatten. A 12mm diameter pipe will give you a width of around 35mm, more than enough for the depth of the chuck's jaws. The copper may benefit by softening, doing this by heating to red heat and allowing to cool naturally.

First, tidy up the recess already made in the end originally supported by the tailstock centre. DO NOT though re-machine the outer rim or the accuracy of the square will be lost. Reverse the part inthe chuck and face the other end, but as the diameter being turned varies from zero in the centre to 24mm at the outside, setting the speed is very much a compromise. Stopping to change the speed is not an option. It is the one process where the

6. Chamfering the top of the cylindrical square. Note the use of copper strip to protect the part.

speed of the lathe should be higher than the outer diameter would suggest, I would suggest at least twice the speed, in this case 1000 to 1200 rpm. Next make a substantial chamfer (speed back at 600 rpm), the purpose of which is primarily to easily identify the non working end of the square **Photo 6**. You will note from this photograph that I have taken the precaution of using a tailstock centre as support for the part whilst making the chamfer. With the cut being quite wide (around 4mm) as the chamfer reaches size the precaution is probably justified, but with a sharp tool and a light feed no doubt it could have been overlooked. I should add that the purpose of the part being supported by the centre is in the interest of finish and not of safety. With the part so far out of the chuck and a wide

cut chatter may set up resulting in a poor finish.

This has been a lengthy item for something outwardly so simple, you will though be much more knowledgeable regarding your machine. If you found adjustments were necessary, then future work will be much more problem free, as attempting to do precision work on a poorly set up lathe can be a frustrating business.

Whether you use your little piece of round steel is up to you. **Photo 7** shows how it can be used to set up a piece of steel in the vice prior to machining. This can be easier than using a small square that would most likely slip between the vice jaws. Two squares, drilled through to take a stud for mounting on the milling machine table, can be used as a substitute for an angle plate. Very useful

7. Using the cylindrical square to set a part upright in the vice.

for machining a new precision angle plate.

The Tailstock Effect

Having now a lathe that will turn parallel it is necessary to consider the effect of a poorly adjusted tailstock. This will be the subject for the next chapter.

Chapter 4

A Between-centres Test Bar

Having ensured that the lathe is set up to turn accurately parallel (as described in Chapter 3), the reader may feel that it would be the end of the subject, this is not so. It is possible that the tailstock could be off centre resulting in work being tapered when the tailstock centre is used to support the workpiece.

Before turning a test piece to check the situation, both centres must be checked for concentricity. Place each in turn in the headstock, after having scrupulously cleaned centres and internal bore. Turn the lathe by hand and check with a dial test indicator that the centre runs true, **Photo 1**. Mark the centre with a spot of marking blue so that it can be seen when a complete rotation has been made. If, as is most likely, both run true (at least better than 0.005mm total indicator reading) all's well. Should however the soft centre be at fault it, can be turned in situ in the headstock. The hardened centre will need grinding, not a

job for the majority of home workshops and it is probably better to purchase a new one. If both are out of true you should suspect the lathe mandrel's bore, hopefully it is just a small dent on the entry to the socket that can be removed with a scraper.

Many lathes have a method of moving the tailstock bodily across the lathe's axis to provide the facility of producing tapered work, though no more than a degree or two. As this permits the centre to be off-centre it must also be used to get it back on the lathe's axis. If this adjustment is not available then it will be a major fitting exercise to correct any fault and this is well beyond the scope of this book, especially as the method will vary from one lathe type to another. Even if the adjustment is not provided the following test piece should still be produced. This will first prove that the tailstock is sufficiently accurate, the most likely case, and secondly the test piece produced will be an essential accessory in later chapters.

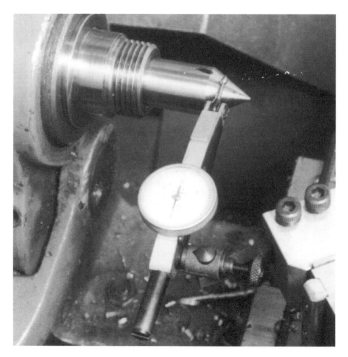

1. Before you undertake serious work you must be sure that both your hard and soft centres run true. Use a dial test indicator with each centre in turn mounted in the lathes spindle, turning this by hand.

Turning the test piece

Cut a 152mm length of 25mm diameter mild steel and centre drill the ends. There are many ways of doing this and the method chosen will depend on the level of accuracy required, and of course the equipment available. For this application I would suggest the simplest, as any error present will be machined out due to the part being machined over its complete length.

If you have a "centre square" then use this to locate the centre, otherwise, using the "Mini height Gauge" as follows is a good alternative. Set the height to 12.5mm as accurately as can be achieved. Mark both ends of the bar with marking blue and place it on the surface plate or some other reasonably flat surface. Scribe a line on the

end, rotate the bar about 120 degrees and scribe again and a further 120 degrees and scribe a third time. If your 12.5mm was spot on then the three lines will cross in the exact centre. If however there was a small error the centre of the bar will be in the centre of the small triangle that the lines produced. Centre punch the end and centre drill to about 5mm diameter on the drilling machine making sure the bar is accurately upright whilst being drilled. Repeat the process on the other end.

With the piece mounted in the 3-jaw chuck and the outer end supported by the tailstock centre, face the end as close to the centre as the tool being used will permit. If you have a "half centre" then use this. Follow this by machining the reduced

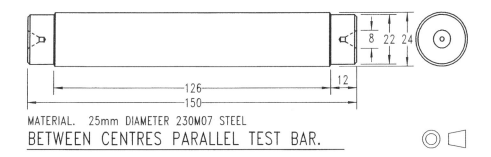

MATERIAL. 25mm DIAMETER 230M07 STEEL

BETWEEN CENTRES PARALLEL TEST BAR.

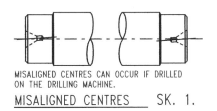

MISALIGNED CENTRES CAN OCCUR IF DRILLED
ON THE DRILLING MACHINE.

MISALIGNED CENTRES   SK. 1.

diameter. If you have a tool that presents an angled leading edge, then use this, it will give a less abrupt transition between the reduced and full diameters than would a 90degree knife tool, (see test bar drawing). Reverse the part and produce the reduced diameter on the other end, as this time it is being held on the now machined portion, do protect this from damage.

As the part has a long term application, a fact that will be understood as the chapters progress, it is desirable that the centred ends are dead in line with each other. SK 1 shows, much exaggerated, the error that could have occurred as a result of them being drilled on the drilling machine. To eliminate this possibility the centres will now be trued on the lathe. With the part still in the chuck from the last operation, remove the centre and fit the fixed steady in a position to locate on the reduced diameter, re-engage the centre to prevent the part moving whilst the steady's arms are fixed in place. Remove the centre and, with a centre drill in the drill chuck deepen the drilled impression to about 10mm diameter. This action will, sufficiently for this case, eliminate any error that may have existed in the alignment of the centre. It will also remove any unmachined end due to facing the end whilst using a full centre. With the first end now centred accurately, reverse the part and centre drill the second using the same sequence of operations.

The part must now be located between centres so that its outside diameter can be

2. *Turning a test bar between centres to check that the tailstock is set accurately on the lathe's axis.*

turned along its length. Do remember to fit the hard centre in the tailstock. Fit the driving dog onto one end of the test piece using some protection to prevent damage to the already machined end.

Whilst turning between centres the peg on the drive plate acts against the arm of the driving dog to keep the workpiece rotating. If the part is not round, maybe when turning a round portion on a square bar, the cut will be intermittent and the drive dog will bounce about on the drive peg, this is not ideal. With a continuous cut the problem is much less, but can still occur with light cuts. It is therefore good practice in all cases to tie the arm on the dog to the drive peg on the drive plate by some means. This can be using some strong twine or copper wire.

When using centres it is good practice to very slightly over advance the tailstock (and I do mean very slightly) to ensure that both centres are fully home, always having first thoroughly cleaned both centres and their sockets. With this done release the pressure and readjust to a running position, do not forget the oil. The part is now ready to have its outer diameter turned along its length. For this operation it is highly desirable that an auto fine feed is set up making it probable that a better finish will result. It will also make the task less laborious as the part is going to be turned along its length a number of times.

Your lathe manual should quote the changewheel combinations for a range of fine feeds. From this choose something between 0.10mm and 0.15mm, much finer than that is unnecessary. Unless you are going to do a lot of rough turning it is this one that is best left set up on the machine. If you do not have a change wheel chart then select the three smallest gears as drivers and the three largest as driven gears, you may have to experiment to find the best order.

Fine Feed Quantified

If you want to quantify the feed rate it will be:- (Dr1 x Dr2 x Dr3 x leadscrew pitch) divided by (Dn1 x Dn2 x Dn3) where Dr are the drivers and Dn the driven. Do take note that if you have an imperial leadscrew, leadscrew pitch is equal to 1 divided by leadscrew TPI. If you are in the fortunate position of having a lathe with a quick change gearbox then you will have the opportunity to easily experiment with differing feeds. Certainly, with the round nose finishing tool, rates faster than 0.15mm are worth trying.

First, using a knife tool, machine along the length with cuts of 0.1mm deep, repeating this till the part has a constant depth cut. At this diameter 600rpm or thereabouts is a good speed to try. No matter how careful you were at centring the part it is likely to run slightly out of true to begin with (the truing of the centres above only made them accurate with each other and the reduced diameter ends). With the part now fully machined replace the knife tool with the finishing tool used on previous occasions. With this take a cut of 0.05mm depth, **Photo 2**, and measure along its length. If already parallel, and we are looking for no more than 0.002mm difference end to end, your lathe is already set accurately. It is though more likely that the tailstock will need adjusting. Inspection

of the tailstock should make it obvious how this is made, if not, then consult the lathe's manual.

Continue to make adjustments and take further cuts of 0.05mm deep until the part becomes parallel. Do now take further light cuts endeavouring to get to 24mm diameter say +/- 0.004mm. Whilst not crucial, having a simple dimension as its diameter may prove beneficial when the test piece is put to use in future applications. The very fine edge on the finishing tool will quite quickly deteriorate, if therefore you make many cuts to get to this point the edge may well require honing again.

Do remember that during this machining sequence the part will warm up and expand, resulting in the need for the tailstock to be reset from time to time. As the cuts taken are only light, temperature rise will be low but tailstock adjustment should nevertheless be checked. For more arduous operations the effect can be extreme and the tightening of the centre in the drilled end due to expansion can cause localised heating that can destroy the centre. Do therefore keep checking adjustment and renewing the lubrication. You should of course not make adjustments whilst a cut is being taken. Also remember that a break in proceedings can cause the part to cool and contract, similarly making adjustment necessary.

During this machining operation do not move the tailstock along the lathe's bed but remove and replace the test piece by advancing and retarding the barrel. The reason for this is that the barrel may not be exactly parallel with the lathe's axis. Remember that all components have an allowable machining tolerance, even super

3. The test bar, turned between centres will, after having been made to prove the tailstock's accuracy, find other uses in setting up the lathe. Treat it as a precision item and store away safely.

precision items, so that this does not necessarily indicate a fault in the lathe's manufacture. The effect of this would be that the centre would not be on the same axis if the extension of the barrel was different to that on the previous pass of the cutter. An important point to take note of here is that the lathe may not turn parallel in subsequent applications if the barrel extension is different and small adjustments may need to be carried out each time a very critical item is turned. The process just carried out will though have familiarised you with the theory. In any case, my concern for the accuracy of the alignment of the barrel is probably unfounded in most cases, as the lathe being used will be sufficiently accurate for it not to be a problem. You do not need to wait though for experience to be gained over a number of applications to see how the lathe performs in this direction, it can be determined with the test piece just made.

With the test piece in place and the barrel in the same position as it was when the test piece was machined, move a dial test indicator along its length with its plunger on the front edge and deflection of the indicator should be minimal. Now carry out the same test with the barrel fully

extended and with it fully retracted. If in both cases the indicator pointer remains essentially static along the length, the tailstock can be considered sufficiently accurate.

Without going into a lot of detail regarding its uses, one application for the test piece can be to use it for setting the top slide accurately parallel with the lathe's axis using a similar approach. This is better than turning a test piece using a turn, measure, adjust, turn, measure, adjust approach.

Whilst there is very little to see resulting from the two items made in the chapters on parallel turning, (just two pieces of parallel steel), the experience and knowledge of the lathe's capabilities should be invaluable. The "cylindrical square" may not be that useful an item but you can use it to check your smaller squares as its accuracy will be greater than workshop grade squares The between centres test bar seen in **Photo 3** will though be immediately invaluable in the next chapter. In this, it will be found possible to turn parts with next to no detectable error in diameter, though as will be illustrated this can only be within the capabilities of ones measuring equipment.

Chapter 5

Hole Gauges

We have so far concentrated on straight forward outside diameter turning and facing where diameter and length have been relatively unimportant. In this chapter the project aims for diameters to be virtually error free, at least within the capabilities of the measuring equipment to be used. Chapter 6 will similarly deal with error free length. To provide the need for producing very accurate outside diameters the chapter deals with hole gauges. Whilst this is a quick and simple project, it needs precision as great as any likely to be needed in the average home workshop.

Precision, the problems

Above all there are two situations that affect our ability to produce parts to a very precise diameter.
1. The sharpness of the tool used.
 2. Being able to feed the tool into the work by very small and precise increments.

Whilst the lathe itself will play a part, even old and worn machines can produce accurate work, especially for smaller items. There is though one aspect of the machine's condition that is important, that is the adjustment of the lathe's bearings and sliding surfaces. These must be adjusted to be free of any play as this would permit the tool to take up differing positions relative to the workpiece from cut to cut.

Tool

As we are endeavouring to make parts that have errors in diameter of no more than -0.0025mm + 0.0000mm, better if possible, we will be taking some very shallow cuts to achieve the final dimension. Typically to reduce the diameter by 0.0025mm the cut will have to be set to 0.00125mm. The essential requirement for taking extremely light cuts is the type and state of the tool used. I think it is obvious that for a very

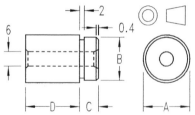

MAKE DIM "B" SMALLER THAN "A" BY
PREFERRED AMOUNT, 0.2mm SUGGESTED

A	C	D
7.000	5	10
8.000	5	11
10.000	6	13
12.000	6	15
14.000	7	17
15.000	7	18
16.000	8	19
20.000	8	23

MATERIAL 230M07 STEEL, DIAMETER TO SUIT

METRIC HOLE GAUGES.

THIS SECTION SHOULD TAPER FROM 6.000
WITH AN INTERNAL ANGLE OF ABOUT
1 DEGREE. THIS WILL THOUGH DEPEND ON THE
ACCURACY OF THE HOLES IN THE GAUGES
WHICH SHOULD PREFERABLY BE REAMED.

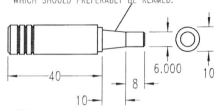

MATERIAL
10mm DIAMETER 230M07 STEEL

HANDLE

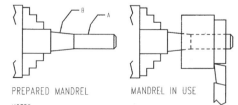

PREPARED MANDREL   MANDREL IN USE

NOTES
A. THIS SHOULD BE A VERY CLOSE SLIDING FIT IN, AND AS LONG, OR ALMOST
AS LONG, AS THE LONGEST PART TO BE MACHINED.
B. THIS TAPER SHOULD HAVE AN INTERNAL ANGLE OF BETWEEN 1 and 2
DEGREES. WHERE MULTIPLE PARTS ARE TO BE HELD THEY MUST ALL HAVE
THE SAME INTERNAL DIAMETER HOLE, A REAMED HOLE IS PREFERRED.
PRECISE CONCENTRICITY CAN ONLY BE ACHIEVED IF THE MANDREL IS TURNED
AND USED WITHOUT REMOVING FROM THE CHUCK
THE MANDREL CAN BE REUSED WHERE CONCENTRICITY IS LESS IMPORTANT.

MAKING AND USING
A TAPER STUB MANDREL   SK 5

1. Using a tool with a very fine edge and a very shallow cut in the order of 0.0005mm grinding dust like swarf is produced. The tool is in need of demagnetising.

shallow cut to be taken, the tool must be honed to have a very fine cutting edge. There will be no point in attempting a cut of 0.0012mm deep if the tool has a radius on its cutting edge of 0.005mm, as the tool will just rub, though it would happily take a cut of say 0.05mm. The tool I use is a round nose tool ground from high speed steel, which I use as it is not possible to get the required cutting edge with tungsten carbide tooling due to the materials make up.

An inexperienced lathe user could be forgiven for considering that a new tip for a replaceable tipped tool would be the answer. Many are though deliberately supplied with a minute radius on their cutting edges to give them strength for heavy duty production work.

The tool I use is the finishing tool first described in Chapter 2, SK 2. However, when used for precision work, rather than finishing the essential factor is that the tool must be honed to a super fine edge. Even so, with it sharpened and ready for use, this should be limited to just the last few finishing cuts as such a fine edge can soon be lost. Because of this, all preparation work should be done with a conventional knife tool. It is worth noting that even though the tool is fed right to left the rake on this tool is front to back and can as a result only take very limited depth cuts, it can of course also be fed left to right.

Another important requirement is that the tool must not be above centre height as in this situation the workpiece will just rub on the front face of the tool and refuse to cut. The reason should be obvious, but SK 1 will help to make it abundantly clear. The outcome of having the tool only just too high is that the cut can be intermittent, that is, as the tool traverses the cut will

53

2. Setting the top slide to an angle of 1 in 100 enables fine cuts to be taken. Typically, a feed of 0.02mm on the top slide advances the tool radially towards the workpiece by 0.0002mm

randomly change from satisfactory to unsatisfactory. This especially may develop when machining small diameter items that may flex as a result of the cutting pressure. Because of this it is best to deliberately set the tool a very little below centre to be sure, say 0.05mm. Also, the characteristic is not just limited to tools specifically for finishing as any tool taking a light cut can exhibit the same result. A similar intermittent cut can result if a tool is in need of sharpening.

Infeed method

Having a tool that will take such a shallow cut serves little purpose if it cannot be advanced with certainty in equally small increments. This is impossible to do reliably by the use of the cross slide and its micrometer dials therefore some other

means has to be used. The easy way of achieving this is to set the top slide at a small angle such that a relatively large axial movement of the top slide results in a much smaller radial movement towards the workpiece. For a large magnification, an angle of 0.6degrees will increase the depth of cut by 0.001mm, for a movement of the top slide of 0.1mm a factor of 100 times. For a lower magnification, an angle of 6 degrees will give a factor of 10. If you are sceptical regarding the ability to take such fine cuts I have included **Photo 1** that shows fine fragments, more like grinding dust, adhering to the end of the tool that is in need of demagnetising.

If your top slide rotation is calibrated, this should be adequate for setting 6 degrees, but setting the angle to 0.6

3. The finished hole gauges which need to be made to very precise diameters.

degrees by this method is impracticable. This is where our between centres test bar (Chapter 4), comes into play. Set this up between centres and with a dial test indicator mounted on the top slide, adjust this until it runs parallel with the test bar SK 3/1. This is also the way to set the top slide accurately for normal turning and is much quicker than the trial and error method.

Now cut a piece of flat steel 110mm long, size not that important but would suggest 40 x 5mm and scribe lines on the top surface 100 mm from each end, see SK 2. Mount this on the top slide with its long edge against the test bar and clamp it in position using the tool mounting clamp, SK 3/2. With this done the top slide can be rotated such that one end of the bar is touching the test piece and the shank of a 1mm diameter drill is held between the flat bar and the test bar at the 100mm mark,

SK 3/3. This can easily be done by winding the cross slide in until the drill becomes just captive and the slide then clamped in this position. **Photo 2** show the top slide being set by this method. The procedure is not limited to setting the top slide to 0.6 degrees but could be used for any precise angle providing the diameter of the spacer is worked out accurately (SK 4).

Hole gauges

Photo 3 shows the completed gauges having diameters of 7, 8, 10, 12, 14, 15, 16 and 20mm. Front left is the handle on which they are mounted whilst being used, and on the right the mandrel on which they are turned. The gauges have a short reduced diameter portion, 0.2mm below gauge size, to give indication that the hole being made approaches the required size, with the front end also having a small chamfer for earlier indication. The chamfer is dimensioned at

55

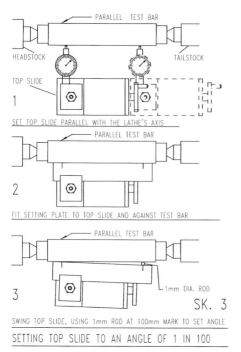

PARALLEL TEST BAR

HEADSTOCK   TAILSTOCK

TOP SLIDE

1

SET TOP SLIDE PARALLEL WITH THE LATHE'S AXIS

PARALLEL TEST BAR

2

FIT SETTING PLATE TO TOP SLIDE AND AGAINST TEST BAR

PARALLEL TEST BAR

3   1mm DIA. ROD

SK. 3

SWING TOP SLIDE, USING 1mm ROD AT 100mm MARK TO SET ANGLE

SETTING TOP SLIDE TO AN ANGLE OF 1 IN 100

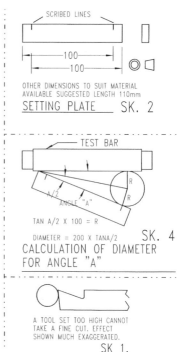

SCRIBED LINES

|——100——|
|—100—|

OTHER DIMENSIONS TO SUIT MATERIAL
AVAILABLE SUGGESTED LENGTH 110mm
SETTING PLATE   SK. 2

TEST BAR

R

A/2   R
ANGLE "A"

TAN A/2 X 100 = R

DIAMETER = 200 X TANA/2   SK. 4
CALCULATION OF DIAMETER
FOR ANGLE "A"

A TOOL SET TOO HIGH CANNOT
TAKE A FINE CUT. EFFECT
SHOWN MUCH EXAGGERATED.
SK 1.

0.4mm which with the reduced diameter at this point makes its leading diameter 1mm less than gauge diameter. The shallow groove between the two diameters ensures that the gauge's main diameter has a clearly visible leading edge.

For economy of material and effort the gauges are made to fit to a common handle the fit achieved by the portion that goes into the gauge being very slightly tapered and a close fit in the hole. For this reason it is essential that the holes are all the same diameter, a reamed hole will be ideal but all holes drilled with the same drill should suffice.

Taper Stub Mandrel

The "taper stub mandrel" is very similar to the handle but rather more critical and is shown on the right of the photograph. Various forms of work holding mandrel are used in lathe work, too many to discuss here, but the taper stub mandrel is probably the most useful and the most simple. Its essential features are, a parallel portion that is a close sliding fit in the hole of the part it is to hold and from the parallel portion, the mandrel tapers to a larger diameter on which the part is pushed. This results in a tight fit giving it the drive necessary for the required machining to take place. A suggested internal angle for the taper is 1 degree, though the angle is not that critical but note that if made too shallow it may not cope with small variations in hole diameters

56

where more than one part is to be held.

The main benefit of this mandrel is that if made, and then the part to be machined fixed onto it without it having been removed from the chuck, then any machining carried out on the workpiece will be precisely concentric with the bore. Similarly work on the end face will also be true to the bore. Whilst removing and replacing the mandrel in a 4-jaw chuck will enable it to be returned with reasonable accuracy, it will never have the degree of precision of a mandrel turned and used at one operation. Where concentricity is important, a taper stub mandrel is frequently the only practical method to achieve the required result. In this case, concentricity is of no importance so the mandrel can be removed and returned.

Making the gauges

Like most machine shop operations there are many ways of achieving the same result, and in this case it may appear a good approach to drill a hole in a piece of material, parting it off and then doing all the remaining work whilst mounted on the mandrel. An accurately made mandrel is capable of providing a fair level of drive making quite heavy machining operations possible. However, the requirement to make the groove in the outer diameter is likely to prove too much, especially as the mandrel is only 6mm diameter.

Place a length of material in the chuck and face the end, centre drill to a little over 6mm and drill and ream (or drill only) 6mm diameter to a depth a millimetre or two longer than the gauge being made. If using a reamer its taper lead will prevent the hole being reamed to its full depth, it will therefore need to be finish reamed after

parting off. Use the parting off tool to make the groove and follow this by parting off to the required length. If the part is being made from bar that is appreciably larger than the gauge being made then the outer diameter can also be reduced prior to parting off. Reverse the part in the chuck and face the end to give the finished length. Use the centre drill to make a small chamfer on the hole. The elimination of the sharp edge on the hole will assist in fitting the part to the stub mandrel. Make all the required gauge sizes to this stage before moving to the next operation.

Making the Mandrel

As the accuracy of the angle for this is not that critical there is no need to go through the detailed process for setting the 100:1 ratio for accurate turning, somewhere between 0.5 and 1.0 degrees (1 to 2 degrees internal) should suffice. If you are not too sure of your top slide's calibration then turn and measure the result before you arrive at the 6mm diameter to fit the gauges. An increase on diameter of around 0.2mm over a length of 10mm should suffice.

Place a piece of steel in the chuck, say 8mm diameter and with some 35mm projecting and, having set the top slide angle, turn a short portion of taper, diameter of no importance. Measure to check that the taper falls within the above limits. Having done that turn diameter "A" say 25mm long (see SK 5) to a little over 6mm also perform preliminary work on the taper. Using the angle of the top slide to reduce the diameter, but winding it back, will enable small changes to be easily made until a very close sliding fit in the gauges holes result. Of course use the saddle for traversing the cutter. On the final cut, achieving the fit and length required for "A", continue by traversing the top slide to finish the taper "B".

Now that the mandrel has been made it will be necessary to remove it for setting the top slide to 0.6 degrees, set the angle such that the top slide being advanced reduces the diameter as seen in **Photo. 2**. Now return the mandrel and fit the largest gauge to it and, using a twisting action as it is fitted to obtain sufficient grip, machine the outer diameters to about 0.3mm above gauge diameter, doing this with a right hand knife tool. Replace this with a finishing tool and using the angled top slide to set the depth of cut, traverse the tool using the saddle. Make repeated cuts until the required diameter is achieved. I suggest that you should aim at size +0.0 - 0.0025mm, preferably better, **Photo 1** shows the result. The accuracy achieved will of course depend on the quality of the measuring equipment available so do check that the micrometer zeros correctly before taking any measurements.

With the outer diameter finished do not move the top slide but feed the cross slide by 0.1mm and finish the smaller diameter. This is less critical than the major diameter and using the cross slide will be sufficiently accurate. Providing free cutting steel is used the finely honed tool should hold its edge long enough to machine the complete set of gauges. If in doubt however, do remove the tool and re-establish the edge before completing the batch.

As you are machining diameters from 7mm to 20mm, a ratio of almost 3:1, do take note that machine speeds should be varied accordingly. I will not quote any speeds as by now you should be getting to grips with the requirement but would add that at these light finishing cuts a slightly higher speed than for heavier cuts at the same diameter could be tried.

Finally, set up a chamfer tool and wind it into the outer edge of the smaller diameter until it just touches, note the cross slide dial setting and continue feeding the tool in for an amount equal to 0.4mm. This makes the smaller diameter of the chamfer 1.0mm smaller than the main diameter and can be used as an early indication of the hole size.

The Handle

The handle is made in the same manner as the stub mandrel but the 6mm diameter is made shorter so that it does not extend beyond the end of the shortest gauge. This will be preferable if a gauge is ever used to check a blind hole.

If you feel disinclined to make the gauges may I add that use for some of the sizes will occur in a number of projects in the book.

Precision in length

In the next chapter precision will again be the subject but this time relating to length rather than diameter, the project being distance gauges.

Terminology

Axial. In line with the axis of a part or machine.

Radial. Items, or movement, radiating from the axis of a part or machine, typically the spokes of a wheel.

Chapter 6

Distance Gauges

Precision in length is less frequently a necessity, possibly because it is more difficult to achieve so the requirement is designed out in many projects. However, what is about to be proposed requires an accuracy as great as that we attempted in making the hole gauges in Chapter 5. The items in question are distance gauges, what could be called "poor man's slip gauges". Essentially these are short tubular lengths of steel whose lengths have been made to very precise values.

The complete set that I have made is seen in **Photo 1** and can be used to measure gaps from 0.5mm up to 25.5mm in increments of 0.5mm and up to 40mm in increments of 1mm. These ranges use no more than three gauges and can be extended if this number is increased, two of each size is made. Using feeler gauges additionally would enable increments of less than 0.5mm to be measured. The

photograph also shows at the rear, a thin piece collet used in the manufacture and front, left and right, the mandrel and adapter tubes for machining the gauges.

My aim was to make the gauges to a tolerance of + 0.0 - 0.0025mm, (preferably better), being the same as for the hole gauges. As I shall explain later, I did not quite achieve this. The method of working is essentially the same as that for the hole gauges, with the use of left and right handed high speed steel knife tools honed to a very fine edge tool enabling minute cuts to be taken. These are set by using the top slide set to an angle of only 0.6 degrees from the cross slide.

Setting the top slide to this angle may present a problem as on some lathes it cannot be fully rotated 360 degrees. This can frequently be overcome by the use of a suitable plate between cross and top slide the general principle of which is shown in

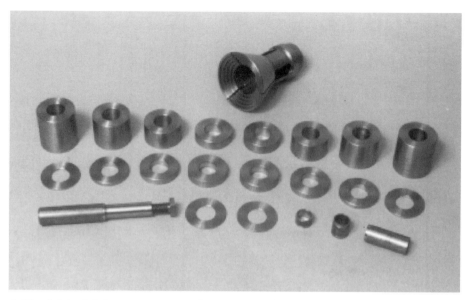

1. The finished distance gauges made to very precise lengths

SK 1. This raises the top slide but a small knife tool sharpened from 3mm square high speed steel would be more than strong enough with such fine cuts being taken.

Even my Myford Super 7 could not be used at the required angle despite the top slide having a full 360 degrees rotation. This was because its operating handle fouled the cross slide preventing the handle from turning, I suspect this would be the case with most lathes. To overcome this the normal handle was temporarily replaced with a small knob, as can be seen in **Photo 2**.

Making the gauges

Making a large number of similar small items can be very wasteful in material as a short unusable part is left in the chuck each time after having made one, or a few, short parts. A way of overcoming this is to use a

fixed steady that allows longer pieces of material to be worked on, the steady then being moved along the bed as the bar becomes shorter. This is one of the major uses for a steady.

Setting a fixed steady

Setting a fixed steady is always a crucial operation and when so far from the chuck more so. The problem is that even if the bar is running true so far from the chuck, and that is unlikely, the bar can easily deflect under pressure from the first arm set. With most lathe steadies the problem can be relatively easy overcome by first setting the steady on the bar whilst mounted close to the chuck. It can then be slid along the bed to its operating position. This requires for the steady to be accurately located on the bed so as to maintain its position as it is moved. Most lathes have steadies that meet this requirement.

As seen in **Photo 3** the operation is being carried out using a 3- jaw chuck, also a potential problem creator. These chucks are not totally accurate and the bar can be off centre when tightened. In some cases, by quite a lot if the chuck is either old and worn, or from the cheaper end of the market. The result of this is that the steady's arms will be set to suit the bar as it sits stationary but as the bar rotates under power the bar will want to take up a new position but the steady will attempt to restrain it. If the steady is moved along the bed where the bar will have a degree of flexibility, even at this diameter, the forces developed will not be that great and can probably be tolerated, depending on the degree of error of course.

With the steady close to the chuck however, the forces will be considerable and as the part rotates these will act on the chuck's jaws in turn. The result of this is for the part to gradually work out of the chuck. I have seen a part move from the

2. The top slide set to an angle of 1 in 100 relative to the cross slide for machining the distance gauge lengths. A special top slide operating knob had to be made as the normal handle fouled the cross slide when set to this angle.

3. The fixed steady being used when making the blanks for the distance gauges. This avoided material wastage that would occur if one, or just a few, parts was made from a short piece of metal mounted in the chuck.

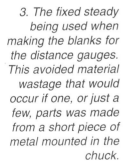

chuck by as much as 6mm in a matter of a minute or two's running. Having had the good fortune of obtaining a chuck whose accuracy would appear to be above average, I have tended to overlook the alternative as far as the photographs are concerned. If you have a 3-jaw chuck that exhibits a total indicator reading of more than say 0.02mm then the 4-jaw should be used and set up to run true.

With the bar mounted in the 3 or 4-jaw chuck fix and adjust the steady close to the chuck. With this done loosen it from the bed and slide to a position just short of the end of the bar, **Photo 3**. First, face the end followed by centre drilling, drilling 6mm diameter and parting off just longer than the gauge to be made. Continue making other gauges, moving the steady back towards the chuck as the bar shortens.

Do remember to lubricate the arms and readjust them to compensate for any wear, and expansion due to heat, that may take place. At a distance from the chuck it will be adequate to adjust the top arm only. If you notice that when the lathe is stopped it tends to stop more abruptly than is normal, this indicates that the steady is too tight and is acting like a brake and is in need of adjustment. When you near the chuck, say 100mm and closer, do reset the steady at the chuck jaws once more.

Setting the top slide

Before proceeding further with machining the gauges the top slide needs setting to the 0.6 degree angle relative to the cross slide. Whilst a similar principle to that used for the hole gauges in Chapter 5 there are slight changes and rather than describing the method, SK 2 should adequately illustrate the process. Note that it is first necessary to carry out stages 1 and 2 shown in SK 3 Chapter 5.

Having made all the gauges thus far they have to be mounted onto a mandrel for final machining to length. Rather than the taper stub mandrel used for the hole gauges a parallel mandrel with end screw fixing is used in view of some gauges being too narrow to work adequately on a taper stub mandrel.

The mandrel is detailed on SK 3 and shows that rather than reducing the length of the mandrel as shorter parts are worked on a range of differing length clamping tubes are detailed. The clamping tubes should be made first as, even though concentricity is not important, the mandrel is best left in position when made. The mandrel can be seen front left and the spacers front right of **Photo 1**.

Fit the first gauge and using the left hand tool face the left hand face as far as the mandrel permits. This will leave a small diameter extension on the gauge but it will be removed easily as detailed later. Having faced the left hand end, fit the right hand tool and face the right hand end, this time measuring the width and setting the depth of cut with the top slide and feeding the tool with the cross slide. The 100:1 ratio between top slide feed and depth of cut will make minute adjustments easy. As a safety measure, the saddle should be locked in position as only a gentle nudge could move it along the bed defeating the attempt for accuracy.

When facing the ends do set a depth of cut adjacent to the mandrel using the top slide and machine the end by winding the tool out using the cross slide. This will produce a superior finish to that achieved if winding the tool in. Having completed the

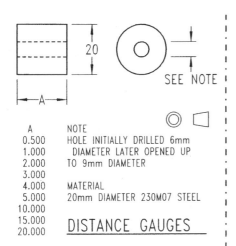

SEE NOTE

A
0.500
1.000
2.000
3.000
4.000
5.000
10.000
15.000
20.000

NOTE
HOLE INITIALLY DRILLED 6mm
 DIAMETER LATER OPENED UP
TO 9mm DIAMETER

MATERIAL
20mm DIAMETER 230M07 STEEL

DISTANCE GAUGES

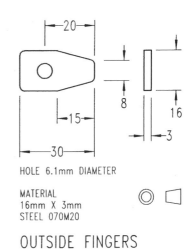

HOLE 6.1mm DIAMETER

MATERIAL
16mm X 3mm
STEEL 070M20

OUTSIDE FINGERS

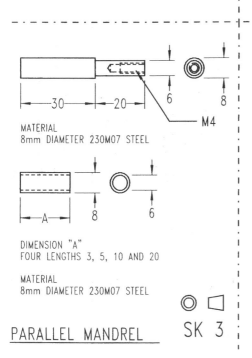

M4

MATERIAL
8mm DIAMETER 230M07 STEEL

DIMENSION "A"
FOUR LENGTHS 3, 5, 10 AND 20

MATERIAL
8mm DIAMETER 230M07 STEEL

PARALLEL MANDREL

SK 3

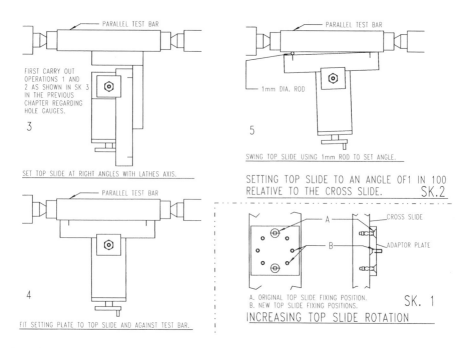

FIRST CARRY OUT OPERATIONS 1 AND 2 AS SHOWN IN SK 3 IN THE PREVIOUS CHAPTER REGARDING HOLE GAUGES.

3

SET TOP SLIDE AT RIGHT ANGLES WITH LATHES AXIS.

PARALLEL TEST BAR

4

FIT SETTING PLATE TO TOP SLIDE AND AGAINST TEST BAR.

PARALLEL TEST BAR

1mm DIA. ROD

5

SWING TOP SLIDE USING 1mm ROD TO SET ANGLE.

SETTING TOP SLIDE TO AN ANGLE OF 1 IN 100
RELATIVE TO THE CROSS SLIDE. SK.2

CROSS SLIDE
A
B
ADAPTOR PLATE

A. ORIGINAL TOP SLIDE FIXING POSITION.
B. NEW TOP SLIDE FIXING POSITIONS. SK. 1

INCREASING TOP SLIDE ROTATION

length, very lightly skim over the outer diameter with the finishing tool to give a professional appearance to the gauges, also, very lightly chamfer both left and right hand corners. Do complete the gauges one at a time, as if all left faces were machined then returned to the mandrel for machining the right hand faces, the gauges may not return to the same position and left and right hand faces may not end up parallel. **Photo's 4 & 5** show the thinnest (0.5mm) and the widest (20mm) being worked on, both on the same mandrel.

Measuring problems

I mentioned earlier that I had failed to make the lengths of the gauges to the tolerance I had wished but any attempt at accuracy can only be as good as the measuring equipment being used. In my case I found it easier to measure the length of the gauges, whilst mounted on the mandrel, with the anvils of the micrometer only about half on the edge of the gauge. This I did, apparently achieving the dimensions I was aiming at. When all the gauges were complete I rechecked their sizes only to find that they appeared to be oversize but on measuring the edge of the gauge it was size, or undersize, as I had wanted. The micrometer was found to have some radial movement at the end of the spindle, obviously giving a variation in the order of 0.01mm between measuring with half and a full anvil. I am now saving up for a reputable metric micrometer.

The error has though led me to consider that I could lightly lap the ends to

4. Using a very finely honed right hand knife tool to achieve the correct width of the 0.5mm gauge whilst held on the mandrel seen bottom left Photo 1.

bring them to dimension, a process that would be a good idea for any reader who want to achieve maximum accuracy. However, this will not eliminate the need to produce accurate results on the lathe as the lapping process is very slow at removing metal, so the initial size must be very close to the required dimension. If lapping the gauges, the aim should be to improve on the accuracy achievable on the lathe.

With the gauges finished thus far they have a small extension in the centre, and on both ends, where it could not be machined away due to the method of holding them on the mandrel. To remove this open up the hole by drilling to 9mm diameter. However, holding the larger gauges in the chuck and drilling, will not present a problem but will be a non starter for the smaller sizes. To overcome this you should use a "thin piece collet" to hold the parts whilst drilling. The one used in my

case is seen at the rear of **Photo 1** whilst **Photo 6** shows it being used to drill the 0.5mm gauge with a 9mm drill. On the basis that such a collet will not be part of the reader's kit it will be back to the collet made in Chapter 2 SK 4. If as suggested, the collet at that time was turned from 25mm diameter material then it can easily be opened up to take the diameter of the gauges, a little under 20mm if the outer diameter has been cleaned up. Place the collet in the chuck complete with the plug in the inner hole to prevent it closing and open up the hole to a good fit on the gauge's outer diameter and to a depth of about 2mm. If you are going down this route then it would be preferable when turning the outer diameter of the gauges to work to a close dimension, say + 0.0 - 0.02mm, as the collet split in just two pieces will be less tolerant of differing diameters than will a three or four way split collet.

Whilst these collets are termed as

5. Using the same mandrel but with a shorter clamp tube, the 20mm gauge is machined to length

6. The thin piece collet (top of Photo 1) holding the 0.5mm gauge whilst it's hole is opened up to 9mm. This removes the small unmachined centre portion left due to it being machined on the mandrel as seen in Photo's 4 and 5.

7. Thin Piece Collet is rather a misleading name, they are quite capable of holding much longer parts for machining, in this case the 20mm long gauge.

8. So that the gauges can be made to check outside dimensions, two small fingers are made for clamping onto one or more gauges using a through screw and nut.

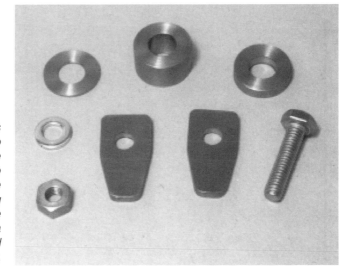

67

"Thin piece collets" their use is not so limited, they can be used for holding much longer items and quite heavy machining carried out. **Photo 7** shows the collet drilling the 20mm long gauge.

Deburr the ends of the holes using hand held countersinking bit, and the gauges are finished. There are though two accessories that are worth considering to extend their use.

Outside dimension fingers

The gauges as made can of course only check distances between the insides of two parallel faces, but by the addition of fingers, as seen in **Photo 8**, outside dimensions can also be checked. This will be helpful when access for a micrometer or a vernier is difficult.

Storage tray

Having given so much effort into producing a precision kit of parts it would be disappointing to see one's efforts destroyed by damage caused through careless storage. A small wooden pegboard is an obvious and simple solution. Make one for the hole gauges also at the same time.

Boring holes

In a number of instances thus far, the need for boring holes has surfaced, thankfully though not too involved as space for more than a passing note or two has not been available. In the next chapter we will be expanding much more on this task that is probably more complex than at first appears to be the case. The project details the making of die holders for use on the lathe, though not to the most commonly available design.

Terminology

Slip Gauges. Small rectangular blocks made in a range of thicknesses, typically 88 in a metric set and made to a high level of precision. By stacking the gauges, sizes can be created in 0.0025mm steps from 2mm up to a few hundred millimetres.

Chapter 7

Tailstock Die Holders

Having dealt thus far with external turning, precision and otherwise, this project primarily deals with boring, but also with turning precision tapers (next chapter).

Boring. The problems!

The task of boring is more fraught with problems than most other turning operations, not least because it is difficult to see the task taking place. The main problem though is the shape of the tool which, because of the internal curvature of the bored hole, reduces the clearance between tool and workpiece. In the case of external turning however, the curvature adds clearance to that of the tool being used. The result is that boring tools are critical to the size of the hole and is particularly a problem with smaller diameters.

Boring small diameters, why?

You may ask, why will it be necessary to bore smaller diameters, say less than 10mm diameter, if I already have drills up to that size and in 0.1mm increments? The reasons are typically:

1. You may have metric drills but want to make a close fitting hole for an imperial spindle. Considering a 3/8in. spindle (0.375in.), the nearest larger size drill will be 9.6mm (0.378 in.), not really a close fit.

2. If a part needs inside and outside diameters to be accurately concentric you may need to bore the inside diameter as drills cannot be guaranteed to start and or continue on axis.

3. A bored hole may be preferable to achieve a better finish.

The tools

If therefore we start on the basis that holes may need to be bored from 6mm up, and smaller is not unknown, then a tool that can cope with that diameter will be required. Commercially available tools at this diameter, if available, are likely to be prohibitively expensive and grinding one from a piece of high speed steel is the only viable option.

This is not the easiest of tasks and needs tackling with considerable caution, due to potential dangers and wasted tool bits if the tool is a failure. The method used to form the cutter will depend on many factors; one's skill, the type of grinder, to name two.

Assuming a simple off hand grinder and only limited experience the sequence in SK 1 will make a good starting point, but before expanding on the subject of forming a cutter we will return to our 6mm boring tool. At this size the tool will be fragile and only light cuts possible, though at 6mm diameter this will not be a problem. Also, being fragile, the depth that the tool can cope with will be limited, say 20mm maximum, rarely a problem as at 6mm. The tool will though cope with ease at larger diameters as the problem of clearance reduces as the hole size increases. However, only being able to take light cuts will make it a frustrating operation, and the 20mm depth limit is likely to be insufficient in many cases. Because of this, larger tools will have to be made, a minimum of three but ideally more.

A tool, made from high speed steel tool bits, will consist of two main features, a reduced size shank as clearance for the hole being bored and the actual cutting head. The critical feature being the shape of the cutter head and how this clears the inside bore it is attempting to make. Endeavouring to put these requirements into words and making them understandable will be a lengthy exercise, SK 2 attempts to illustrate more easily the vital considerations.

Earlier in Chapter 5, the question of tool height was discussed and SK 1 included to show how making a cut would be difficult if the tool were too high. The reverse situation applies to boring tools, here, if a tool is too low, this may cause the cutter to fail to cut properly. With experience you will find that at the cutter's limit, only a small increase in height will change the cutter from a non starter to one that performs with perfection. This feature can be used to advantage where a tool, just too large for the hole size can be pressed into service by mounting it above centre, see SK 3.

Whilst high speed steel tools are the only types practicable at smaller diameters, the deeper holes likely to be required at larger sizes, will demand tools that have a deeper reach than can be achieved with high speed steel tool bits. These, due to their brittle nature make the tool too fragile for deep holes. To overcome this, tools with separate cutter tips will be needed, such as, replaceable tip tools, tungsten carbide tipped tools or just home made holders with small pieces of high speed steel. **Photo 1**, showing a range of boring tools, includes some tooling of this type. For very small diameters, cutters made from round high speed steel bits in diameters of 4, maybe 5mm and fitted in a small mild steel holder make an ideal solution at these sizes. **Photo 1** shows a complete example of this, top but one on the right hand side, with a suitable additional cutter bottom but one. The outcome of all these factors is that for basically the same operation a much wider range of tooling will be required than most will anticipate.

Tailstock die holders

These die holders have been chosen to provide the need for boring operations.

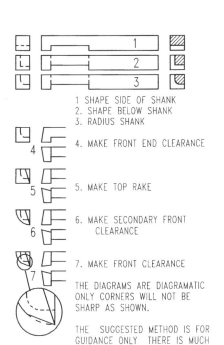

1 SHAPE SIDE OF SHANK
2. SHAPE BELOW SHANK
3. RADIUS SHANK

4. MAKE FRONT END CLEARANCE

5. MAKE TOP RAKE

6. MAKE SECONDARY FRONT
   CLEARANCE

7. MAKE FRONT CLEARANCE

THE DIAGRAMS ARE DIAGRAMATIC
ONLY CORNERS WILL NOT BE
SHARP AS SHOWN.

THE SUGGESTED METHOD IS FOR
GUIDANCE ONLY   THERE IS MUCH
FREEDOM TO VARY METHOD AND
SHAPE TO SUIT.

SK. 1.

SHAPING BORING TOOLS

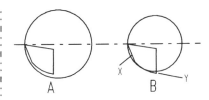

THE BORING TOOL BEING USED IN HOLE "A"
WILL NOT WORK IN THE SMALLER HOLE "B"
EVEN THOUGH THERE IS STILL FRONT
CLEARANCE AT "X" AS THE TOOL FOUL'S
AT "Y"

BORING TOOLS
AND HOLE SIZES   SK. 2.

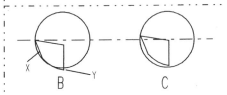

THE BORING TOOL WHICH FOUL'S IN HOLE "B"
WHEN MOUNTED AT CENTRE HEIGHT CAN BE
PRESSED INTO SERVICE IN THE SAME SIZE
HOLE IF RAISED ABOVE CENTRE AS AT "C"

BORING TOOLS
AND TOOL HEIGHT   SK. 3.

BLIND   THROUGH

A THROUGH HOLE TOOL CAN HAVE A LARGER
TIP RADIUS MAKING IT PREFERABLE WHERE
A GOOD FINISH IS IMPORTANT TYPICALLY
FOR A BEARING   SK. 4.

BORING TOOL SHAPES.

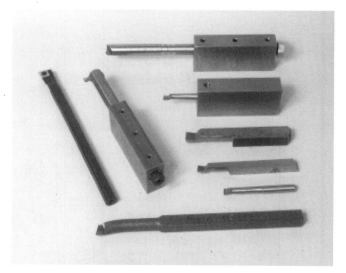

1. Even for basic boring, tools vary depending on diameter, depth and material. This results is far more tools being required than for simple external turning.

Whilst not unique, the design differs from that most common. This has a mounting for the two sizes of die in a single unit, one at each end. The design in this case can easily be observed from **Photo 2**. Its essential differences, and I consider advantages, are the use of a tommy bar and having separate holders for each size of die. The use of a tommy bar avoids the problem of the handle fouling the cross slide, top slide, etc., which can make the operation difficult. Separate holders also

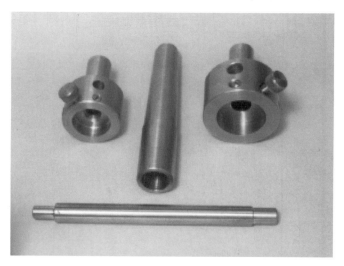

2. One inch and 13/16 inch die holders for use in the lathe tailstock.

allow two differing sizes of thread to remain set up where the parts being made need this. In fact the holders are so simple to make that you could make one for each commonly used thread size leaving the dies permanently fitted.

Two methods

Whilst both holders are essentially the same, I have used a different sequence of operations for each. You may chose to use one, or the other, method for both holders, though if its experience you are after do follow the two methods.

Like many workshop owners I went through a stage where lack of available money and time to make items of tooling, frequently resulted in me using less satisfactory methods. Without taking space

to elaborate, the situation did make me realise the importance of the die aligning with the workpiece accurately, and for this reason I have paid particular attention to this requirement in the two manufacturing methods.

Method one

Method one is used for the smaller holder. Chuck a length of 32mm diameter steel, about 80mm long, and check that the outer end is running true, say within 0.02mm total indicator reading. If this is not achieved in the 3 jaw, use the 4 jaw. With a relatively large diameter and short piece of steel, it should be possible to set up the fixed steady on the outer end without additional support for the workpiece. The problem with longer and or slimmer workpieces is that the first arm applied can deflect the part off axis.

Another fact, so important that I feel I

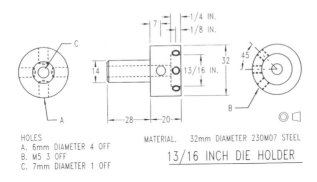

HOLES
A. 6mm DIAMETER 4 OFF
B. M5 3 OFF
C. 7mm DIAMETER 1 OFF

MATERIAL.   32mm DIAMETER 230M07 STEEL

13/16 INCH DIE HOLDER

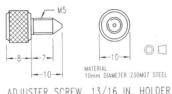

MATERIAL
10mm DIAMETER 230M07 STEEL

ADJUSTER SCREW, 13/16 IN. HOLDER

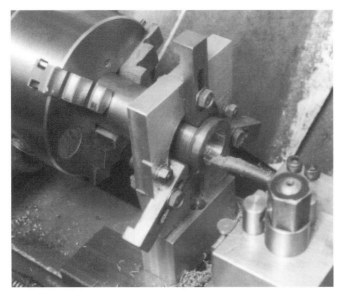

3. The bore for the smaller holder being made.

should again comment, is the problem of attempting to support a part that is not running true at the point at which the steady is being used. As the part rotates it will attempt to follow its natural path but the steady will exert a considerable force as it attempts to restrain the part to run within the steady's arms. This can cause the part to work out of the chuck with the situation becoming more critical the closer the steady is to the chuck. It is particularly crucial if the part is large in diameter and the reverse jaw are being used. It is essential therefore that when using the steady close to the chuck that the workpiece runs true and every effort is made to set up the steady accurately. *Do take note* it is easy to overlook this situation. Please excuse me if I repeat myself but with the book being primarily aimed at the novice some repetition should be beneficial. Face the end of the bar to remove saw cut

marks and drill the end of the bar with the largest drill you have and to a depth just short of the depth of the bore to be made. Depending on the size of the drill you may need to use a smaller drill first to avoid overloading the lathe's motor. You must of course, chose a boring tool that will work at the drilled hole diameter and is able to face the end of the bore. Boring tools as purchased come in two basic forms, though of course there are many variations. These are illustrated in SK 4 and are essentially for blind hole and through hole boring. Personally, whilst I have tools of both types, those I grind from high speed steel tool bits are invariably to suit blind holes, and as the bore in this case is shallow I would normally use a high speed steel tool, such as that third from the top right **Photo 1**. However, you will see from **Photo 3**, that I chose to use a tungsten carbide tipped tool, of a type that are very commonly available.

74

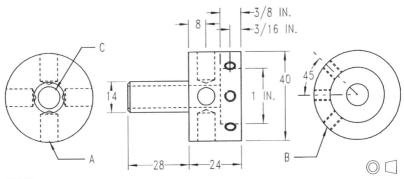

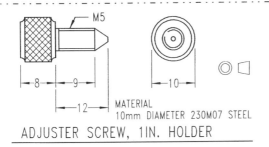

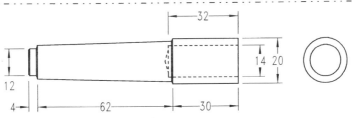

HOLES
A. 8mm DIAMETER 4 OFF
B. M5 3 OFF
C. 10.5mm DIAMETER 1 OFF

MATERIAL.   40mm DIAMETER 230M07 STEEL

1 INCH DIE HOLDER

MATERIAL
10mm DIAMETER 230M07 STEEL

ADJUSTER SCREW, 1IN. HOLDER

THE DIMENSIONS ARE FOR A NUMBER 2 MORSE TAPER FOR
OTHER TAPERS THE DIMENSIONS WILL HAVED TO CHANGE.

MATERIAL   20mm DIAMETER 230M07 STEEL

TAILSTOCK DIE HOLDER SUPPORT

4 and 5. The shank of the smaller holder being made using left and right hand knife tools whilst supported by the tailstock centre.

Start increasing the diameter and boring to a depth of 6.5mm. If you own a "saddle stop" (see Photo 12, Chapter 12) then set this to control the depth using the saddle to feed the tool. Having managed without a saddle stop for many years I soon learnt its considerable advantages once I equipped myself with one, and would urge you to make one as the time will be repaid many times over. Setting the stop is a job for the distance gauges made in chapter 6. Select gauges to the width of 6.5mm (5 + 1 + 1/2) and, using the saddle's advance wheel, grip them between the end of the stop adjusting screw and the saddle. Then, with them in this position, advance the top slide until the tool just touches the face of the part to be bored (lathe not rotating). Remove the distance gauges and the depth of bore will be exactly 6.5mm using the saddle to advance the tool. Do not move the top slide.

If you do not own a saddle stop then it will be necessary to control the depth by observing the top slide dial. Lock the saddle and bring the tip of the boring tool up to the face of the workpiece and zero the micrometer dial. Set the depth of cut using the cross slide and bore to a depth of 6.5mm using the top slide using its dial to set the depth. Continue increasing the diameter until the bore arrives at 13/16in. (dies are made to imperial dimensions). On the final cut feed the boring bar deeper by 0.05mm and wind the boring bar to the centre, by so doing facing the base of the bore. If this does not result in a clean finish place a further cut of 0.05mm and face the base again, repeat as necessary. With a right hand knife tool, machine the outer end face doing this until the depth of the bore measures 1/4in.

Next centre drill the base of the bore followed by removing the steady and

76

supporting the part with the tailstock centre. The next task is to make the 14mm diameter spigot on the rear, first with a left hand knife tool, **Photo 4**, also establishing the 20mm dimension at this stage. Then with a right hand tool, (**Photo 5**) continue to increase the length of the 14mm diameter. To ensure both parts of the spigot are the same diameter, mark the first part with a light ring of marking blue. For the final finishing cut with the right hand tool, this can be advanced until there is just evidence of the tool touching the blue area and the second end turned to finished size. Make the spigot 34mm long to enable parting off to take place at this reduced diameter.

Fit now a finishing tool and use this to skim the 32mm diameter to give a good finish and with a chamfer tool, chamfer both front and rear edges of the major diameter. Finally, part off at 28.5mm long, **Photo 6**,

(note the blue ring mentioned in the previous paragraph) after first drilling 7mm diameter through to this depth.

With the material now shorter the part can safely be held on the 32mm diameter, suitably protected, and the end of the spigot faced to a 28mm length, and finally chamfered. There only remains for the holes for the tommy bars and the die adjusting screws to be made. This is a simple exercise and I will not comment other than to say if you have a dividing head, using this will help to position the holes regularly, though this is not that important, especially those for the tommy bars.

Making the screws should, with the experience now gained, be a relatively straightforward exercise. However, you will need the knurling tool described in Chapter 11 and the use of the die holders now being made. It will therefore be a case of making

6. Parting off the almost finished small holder.

do with conventional screws in the short term.

The larger holder

In design, the holder for the one inch die is only a larger version of the smaller and could therefore use the same manufacturing procedures. However, to gain more experience a different approach is to be described.

Method two

One advantage of this method over that for the smaller holder is that it starts with a piece of material only just long enough for making the part, there being no short stub left therefore which may not find a use. Cut a piece of material 40mm diameter by 53mm long and mount this in the chuck using the reverse jaws if necessary. Unless the outer end is running way out of true you can proceed as follows, otherwise, true up using the method in Chapter 2, Photo 1. Centre drill the end and support with the

tailstock centre, and, using a right hand knife tool, create the spigot, **Photo. 7**. Make it just over 28mm long and oversize at 14.5mm diameter. Face the end of the head to a final finish. Remove the tailstock centre and with care, face the end of the spigot resulting in a length of 28mm. Remove from the chuck and return the normal jaws.

Replace the holder in the chuck, this time holding it on the spigot and face the end making the length of the larger diameter 24.3mm. Follow this by boring the 1 in. diameter, and final finishing the outer face to give 24mm, centre drilling and through drilling the 10.5mm diameter. I have not gone into detail as this is essentially a repeat of the small holder. Do make certain that the base of the bore is faced level.

The next stage is to reduce the spigot to 14mm at the same time ensuring that it is axially in line with the die housing. To make a parallel stub mandrel, place a piece of 30mm diameter steel, around 40mm long, in the chuck, concentricity not at all important. Face the outer end and turn a 1in diameter portion 12mm long, the 1 in. diameter must be a close fit in the bore of the holder and the end sit cleanly on its base. Drill and tap the centre of the mandrel M6.

Fit the holder onto the mandrel and hold in position using an M6 screw and reduce the spigot to 14mm + 0.0 / -0.02mm as seen in **Photo 8**, followed by chamfering the end. With the mandrel having remained in the chuck since it was made the spigot just turned will be accurately in line with the die holding bore. Whilst still on the mandrel the 40mm diameter can be skimmed over for appearance sake and the two ends chamfered. Remove then drill and tap the holes as for the smaller holder.

Keep a store of used mandrels

Whilst the mandrel will not return to the chuck with the same degree of concentricity, even using a 4 jaw chuck, it should be kept for possible future use. It may be of use at 1 in. diameter in a less critical application but more likely it will be turned down for using at a smaller diameter, at least the tapped hole will be ready prepared.

Tommy bar

Do make the ends of the tommy bar a close but easy fit in the holes in the holders this will ensure they do not slide out of the hole in use.

Chapter 8 will deal with making precision tapers and working with screws enabling the taper and the screws to be made to complete the die holders.

7. Turning the larger die holder shank leaving it oversize for eventual finishing.

8. The larger holder shank being finished turned whilst held on a mandrel after boring.

Chapter 8

Precision Tapers

Making precision tapers is an essential feature of two projects in this book and will continue to be if you become involved in making workshop equipment. Being unable in the home workshop to measure the angles involved in precision tapers sufficiently accurately, most adopt a method of trial and error elimination. This consists of making a taper, testing it with its mating item, noting the error, making adjustments, re-machine. A case of machine, test, adjust, re-machine, test, adjust and so on until a satisfactory result is arrived at. Having adopted this method myself many times, I became aware that it was far from ideal, not least because it often required the part being machined to be removed from the lathe to enable it to be tested with its mating half. Because of this I developed the following method.

Its essential feature is the ability to measure two diameters of the taper at two

points a very specific distance apart, from these determining that the angle is set accurately. A test piece is made having two flanges, the distance between their two trailing edges being such that the difference in their diameters must be 0.040in. **Photo 1**. If the taper is to be turned with the smaller end adjacent to the chuck, as in Chapter 13, Photo 2, the distance is between the two leading edges. Having made the test piece it can be retained and reused until the flanges have been turned away, as can be observed by the rusty nature of the test piece in the photograph.

Though I am providing this series essentially in metric dimensions, I do anticipate that the majority of the readers will be working on imperial machines. As the system relies on an easily read difference of 0.040 in., it would make no sense to convert this to a metric value that would be difficult to read, I will therefore

81

1. Turning the test piece for setting the top slide to the correct angle for machining a Morse taper. The test piece can be used many times hence its rusty appearance.

explain the system using imperial dimensions. However, for the benefit of readers with metric machines I am including a table giving distance between edges for a 1mm difference in diameter, do though note that these are not conversions of the imperial values.

The imperial table gives the dimensions of the test piece based on the difference between the smaller and larger diameters being 0.040 in. With the top slide set to give this difference a taper can be turned using the normal outside diameter turning methods.

Even with this method I found that setting the top slide can still be on the difficult side due to the need to make very small adjustments to the angle set, but at least it avoids the turn, remove, test, replace, turn, remove, test, sequence of events. I have though adopted an approach that minimises the problem making the task considerably easier.

Having taken a trial cut leave the tool in contact with the larger diameter and measure the two diameters. For an example let us assume the larger diameter is only 0.039 in. larger than the smaller, thus needing the angle to increase. Loosen the top slide and swing it away from the test piece, move the cross slide forward by 0.001 in. and then rotate the top slide until the tool once again touches the test piece and re-clamp the slide in place. This will have made a small and controlled increase to the angle. You may ask why if the error was 0.001in. on diameter was the adjustment not only 0.0005 in.. The reason being because the change of angle will have an effect on the smaller diameter also.

If the error in the difference was larger than required, again leave the tip of the tool in contact with the larger diameter having made the test cut, but this time, after loosening the top slide, wind out the cross slide and then wind it back in stopping

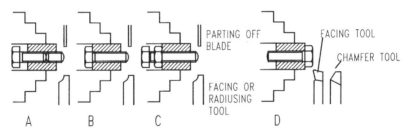

PARTING OFF BLADE

FACING TOOL

CHAMFER TOOL

FACING OR RADIUSING TOOL

A   B   C   D

THESE SKETCHES ILLUSTRATE HOW TO WORK ON SCREWS USING A THREADED
COLLAR TO HOLD THEM, "A" A GRUB SCREW "B" A HEADED SCREW, "C"
A LONGER HEADED SCREW AND "D" MACHINING THE HEAD OF A SCREW.

WORKING WITH SCREWS   SK. 1.

- -

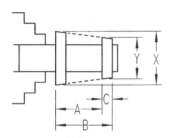

AS DIMENSION "A" WILL BE DIFFICULT TO
MEASURE ACCURATELY MEASURE DIMENSIONS
"B" AND "C"AND TAKE "C" FROM "B" TO
ARRIVE AT "A"

IF MEASURING EQUIPMENT IS AVAILABLE TO
DOUBLE DIMENSION "A" THE DIFFERENCE
(X-Y) CAN BE DOUBLED MAKING AN EVEN
MORE ACCURATE RESULT ACHIEVABLE.

MORSE TAPER / FOOT		DIMENSION "A" FOR	
NO.	ON DIAMETER	X-Y=0.040"	X-Y=1.00mm
1	0.59858"	0.8019"	20.047mm
2	0.59941"	0.8008"	20.020mm
3	0.60235"	0.7969"	19.922mm
4	0.62326"	0.7701"	19.254mm

MORSE TAPER
TEST PIECE DIMENSIONS

2. The Morse taper being machined.

0.001in short of its previous reading. The top slide, then being rotated so as the tool again touches the test piece, will this time be set to a shallower angle. Skim over the test piece once more and again measure, repeat the process until the desired result is achieved. I can guarantee that this process is easier to carry out than to describe.

Taper for the die holders

In Chapter 7 two die holders were made which require a taper on the die holder support. The dimensions on the drawing assume a number 2 Morse taper and will require changing should your lathe's tailstock have a different taper. The chart published gives test piece values for four sizes of Morse taper and shows that a different test piece will be required for each size taper to be made. The reason for the

differing test pieces is that unfortunately each Morse taper has a slightly different taper value.

Another relatively common taper, the "Brown and Sharpe", has a consistent taper for its smaller sizes, that is up to size 9, and is 0.5in. taper in 12in. This results in a test piece requiring flanges 0.96in apart for a 0.40in difference in diameters. If working to metric dimensions the values are 24mm apart for a 1mm difference in diameters. For any other taper you must consult your machine manual and calculate the values.

Having set the top slide at the required angle the process now consists of straight forward outside diameter turning. First, rough turn the taper using a right hand knife tool and then use the finishing tool as is seen in **Photo. 2**. One aspect of turning longer tapers is that the travel of the top

3. Boring the end of the Morse taper to take the die holder shanks.

slide may be too short to finish the taper in one pass. This will be no problem at the roughing stage but can cause a small step in the taper when finishing off. To minimise the effect use the following process. First, finish the smaller end leaving the larger end unfinished over a length that the slide will just cover at one pass. This ensures that if there is a step it is furthest from the working end of the taper, though the following will virtually eliminate the possibility.

Having finished the smaller end apply a very thin layer of marking blue to it adjacent to the unfinished portion. Then, with the lathe running, very slowly advance the finishing tool towards the blue area until there are just signs of the tool touching the taper, then feed the top slide to finish the larger end. This should give a virtually step-less transition between the two areas.

Being your first taper turned using this method it is understandable if you still feel apprehensive regarding the result and wish

to test the finished taper against the bore in which it is to fit. Very lightly mark the taper with marking blue and place it into its mating taper, having first cleaned it thoroughly. With the taper inserted just sufficiently to make full contact but still able to be rotated, rotate the taper one turn and remove. If the taper is correct there will be some evidence of the blue having touched the internal taper at numerous points along the taper's complete length. I think, like me, that after having made a few tapers using the method you will forgo this testing phase as done with care you will find the system foolproof.

Having satisfied yourself that all is OK, again clean both the headstock taper and the taper just made and insert the taper into the headstock and bore to take the die holder shanks as shown in **Photo 3**. Do this by drilling 12mm and boring to 14mm. Use the 14mm hole gauge described in Chapter 5 to size the hole. You may ask why not use the spigot on the rear of the

4. The use of a tommy bar makes operation of the die holder easier than ones that have fixed handles that can foul the top slide, cross slide, etc.

die holder, but as this does not have the reduced diameter portion there will be no early warning that the hole approaches size. Skim the outer diameter for appearance sake, face the end and chamfer and the taper shank is complete.

If your headstock has a larger taper than the tailstock, as is sometimes the case, the following process should be adopted. Initially set your piece of metal in the 4 jaw chuck setting it to run true adjacent to the jaws and turn the taper. This will ensure that the taper is reasonably concentric with the unmachined portion held in the chuck. Having made the taper, remove and replace in the 4 jaw for making the 14mm bore. Leave a little of the outer diameter proud of the chuck's jaws and again set this to run true then make the bore as above. This will ensure that the bore is concentric with the outer diameter that is concentric with the taper.

The die holders are now ready for use as seen in **Photo 4**. Normally I am operating with a rear tool post in position but even with this removed, as in the photograph, the removable tommy bar proved to be a definite asset

Using the die holders.

Having obtained your dies and die holders, how are they used? The first question is, with the lathe under power or turning the die by hand? For the beginner the latter is definitely the approach and in any case is almost always the method to use. I personally almost never use threading dies with the lathe turning. Even for the experienced I would suggest it is only a possibility if using best quality dies with very free cutting materials and for smaller sizes only, say M5 and below. It would then have to be done at the lathes slowest speed.

Preparation of the part to be threaded is minimal, turn the outer diameter to the thread diameter, or very slightly over, say

5. Bottom centre a grub screw slotting jig, together with various items for holding screw whilst working on them in the vice or the lathe.

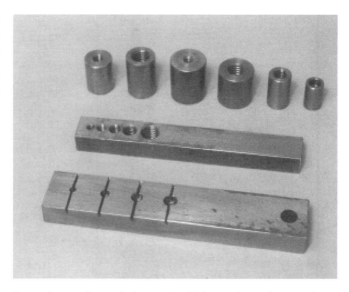

+ 0.02mm to +0.04mm depending on the size of the thread. This gives the die just a little to take off at the crest of the thread rather than just rubbing and will also stop there being a flat on the thread if it wanders a little. A chamfer at the end of the prepared part will aid the die to get off to an acceptable start. Even so, with this done the first thread or two can be below standard, especially with economy dies. If possible therefore, make the part a little on the long side and reduce to length after threading as this will eliminate any poor initial threads. The use of a threading compound is also a good idea.

Dies, having a split in which a pointed screw locates, can be opened up with this, or closed using the two, small grub screws. This means that the die will not automatically cut the correct size when the die is first run down the workpiece, ideally it should be used and set on a test piece before being put to work on the actual part

being made. This can be a chore and one that most would prefer to avoid, so making a holder for each die and keeping it set is often put forward as the approach to take. As I have already found these holders easier to use than my double ended holder, I am very much of a mind to make sufficient holders for all my more frequently used thread sizes, why don't you? it will be good experience. If this seems extravagant then compare this with the multitude of quick change tool holders many readers own and use.

Adjuster screws

To make the adjuster screws for both holders, the holders will need to be fitted with ordinary screws as a temporary measure. With the experience gained so far, making the screws should not present a problem, other than the need for them to be knurled, a process that is covered in Chapter 11. I would suggest therefore that

87

you stay with temporary screws, replacing them with the knurled versions as detailed in the drawings once knurling has been explained.

This still leaves the grub screws that traditionally have been slotted types, if you wish to use socket screws I see no reason why this should not be. However, if you wish to stay with tradition the following gives some guidance on their manufacture.

Working with screws

When working with screws in the home workshop the requirement will invariably be to modify an existing screw to arrive at a variation that fits the specification of the project in hand. This will consist of:-
1. Reducing in length.
2. Changing the head size.
3 Changing the head type.
4 Changing the form of the end, pointed, radiused, etc.
5 Taking a short length from an existing screw slotting the end to make a slotted grub screw.

There are two approaches to these tasks, 1, a purely manual one, hack saw, file, etc., and 2, a machine assisted one, parting off and making a radius on the end, etc.

Let us take requirement 5 first as this task is necessary for our die adjusting screws. For this a slotting jig requires to be made as seen bottom **Photo 5**. It is suggested that, unless a large number of slotted grub screws are required when they should be slotted with a slotting saw on the milling machine, this simple jig will give very good results for small numbers. The aim of the jig is to ensure that the slot is made centrally on the end of the screw as any small error will become visually very apparent.

Take a length of steel, typically 16 x 8mm cross section, and make a number of saw cuts across it to a depth of about 3mm one slot for each size of screw to be catered for. Use a normal junior hack saw blade as this will be a suitable width for most sizes, say M4 to M8. If you are into very small work then a junior hack saw could be thinned over a short length using the off hand grinder. This could then be used with a little extra care on say M2.5 and M3.

With the length of steel slotted take a large centre punch, lodge it in the centre of each slot and make a substantial centre punch mark. After this drill through with a small drill in the order of 1mm diameter. Turn the jig over and then drill with tapping drill sizes for the screw threads you intend to use. Tap the holes as required and the jig is complete.

To make the grub screw take a screw of suitable length and place a nut on it. Thread the screw into the jig from the non slotted side and when flush on the other, lock in position using the nut for the purpose. It is then a simple process to slot the end of the screw using the jig to guide the saw resulting in the slot being accurately placed on the end of the screw. Following this place a length of steel in the 3-jaw, about 15mm long, say 10mm diameter, face both ends and drill and tap to the thread size being worked on. This can then be used to hold the screw for working on, parting off, shaping the end, etc. Rather than going into lengthy descriptions SK1 shows how this simple device can be put to use.

In the next chapter a screw jack provides experience machining cast iron. The jack also requiring screw threads to be cut on the lathe the necessary instruction for this is included in Chapter 10.

Chapter 9

Screw Jack

The subject in this chapter is quite different from those included elsewhere in the book, both in terms of material and processes. Having worked so far with mild steel, this subject is a small screw jack made primarily from cast iron. Whilst all that needs to be said about machining the material can probably be included in a few short paragraphs it will soon be realised that the main problem with castings is their rough shape and how they can be held as a result. The jack, seen in **Photo 1**, also gives the first opportunity at trying one's hand at screw cutting, a process that will be very much to the fore in Chapters 12 and 13.

The casting is obtainable from The College Engineering Supply (Ref. 1) their reference being "511-small". As it is a relatively small casting, non UK readers should not find it prohibitively expensive to import. Whilst referred to as "small" it does need a lathe of at least 75mm centre height

to machine it easily. If you have a smaller lathe you could purchase some cast iron bar, say 40mm diameter and 75mm long and machine a jack from that. This would give experience in turning cast iron and screw cutting but it would not have the same problems as with a rougher casting.

The casting comes with a fully detailed drawing but as will be seen I did make two changes. The top of the spindle could not pivot to cope with surfaces that were not totally parallel, so I modified it as per SK 1. The other was to make a threaded insert rather than threading the casting directly. I considered that the newcomer to cutting threads on the lathe would prefer it this way as a failed internal thread would not mean a scrapped casting.

Machining cast iron

Machining cast iron falls into two stages. The outer skin can be extremely hard and

1. The finished screw jack.

without proper precautions can easily destroy the tool being used. However, with the outer skin removed machining is as easy or even easier than mild steel. It does though machine quite differently and it is a very dirty operation. Do therefore use a good barrier cream on the hands.

Choice of tool type is especially important, do not use a precious high speed steel tool as one hard spot and the tool will be in need of sharpening, so this is really a non-starter unless you have no other choice. I would suggest a tungsten carbide tipped tool as sets of these in varying shapes can be purchased quite economically. Removable tipped tools can also be used but if you wish to use these do ensure the tools you are purchasing are of a suitable grade. Having chosen your tool type, choice of tool shape will follow much the same lines as tools for machining mild steel. For this project, left and right hand knife tools and boring tools will be used.

If you chose brazed, tungsten carbide tipped tools take note that like high speed tools, tungsten carbide tools need sharpening from time to time, albeit less often. The process follows the same basic procedures, use of off hand grinder or dedicated tool and cutter grinder, etc. but requires these to be fitted with special green grit wheels for use on tungsten carbide. These are not over expensive but it does need the wheel to be changed every time you change from high speed steel to tungsten and back. Whilst the process is the same more effort is required to remove the blunt edge. Do not be surprised therefore if it requires more pressure and takes longer to accomplish. Because of this I feel they should not be a first choice for machining mild steel, a point I now realise

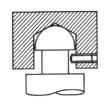

SWIVEL TOP   SK. 1.

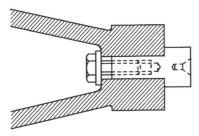

SMALL END PLUG SK. 2.

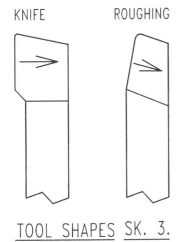

KNIFE   ROUGHING

TOOL SHAPES SK. 3.

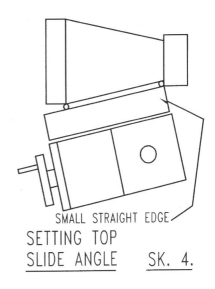

SMALL STRAIGHT EDGE

SETTING TOP
SLIDE ANGLE   SK. 4.

2. The top slide, unusually set with the handle on the left to avoid hitting the tailstock. A deep cut is being taken with ease

I should have made earlier in the book.

Having mentioned the casting's hard surface that can destroy cutters, of any type, care has to be taken to make sure that the method used to machine the component attempts to overcome the problem. It is not though an inevitable obstacle as many castings will machine with ease. The method is to make the first cut sufficiently deep to get below the surface as seen in **Photo 2** though the cut in this is rather deeper than normally needs be, for a reason that I will explain later.

With castings being of irregular shape, a cut that starts sufficiently deep may subsequently just scrape the surface as the machining progresses, a sure recipe for a damaged tool. Under these circumstances the process should be halted and the tool returned to the start and a deeper cut set. However, breaking through the outer surface cannot be avoided totally and **Photo 3** is an example. Here, the right hand knife tool is machining the base of the jack but it is obvious that as each new cut is taken it must first break through the surface layer as it moves right to left.

Having totally removed all the surface skin the remaining machining can proceed with ease as at this stage cast iron is very easy to machine. If the task in hand has some special requirement for which you do not have a suitable tungsten tool, then using a high speed tool for this can proceed with very little more caution than is normal. It is incidentally normal to machine cast iron dry.

The jack

Having dealt with the problems of machining, there frequently remains a much more difficult situation, holding the part. Whereas machining is a common problem for all cases, holding the part varies considerably from project to project. The nature of castings is for them to be a rather irregular shape and this can present extreme problems in establishing a secure method of holding them. On a difficulty scale of one to ten (ten being most difficult)

3. Initial machining of the casting whist held internally on the outer steps of the chucks normal jaws and supported by the tailstock using a plug in the casting's bore.

this casting only comes in at four, even so it has to be approached with care.

The first task is to machine the ends of the casting as already seen in **Photo 3** giving the first opportunity of getting to grips with the part. **Photo 4** shows the casting as received in its unmachined state. A small hole also exists in the top of the casting in preparation for the screw thread. If this is your first encounter with a casting then you will realise perhaps for the first time that this is no precision component, though this does not indicate a second rate product, it is just the nature of the process.

Photo 3 shows that the casting is held primarily on the inside of the hole at the large end, being the first time in the book that the chuck has been used in this way. The inside of the hole will need its rough edges removing using an old, half round file. With this done the hole will not be perfectly round but will be adequate for the task providing it is also supported at the outer end. If you turn the lathe by hand you will find that the outer end runs far from

true this is not at all surprising considering the state of the bore. This error will though be minimised at the next stage.

For supporting the casting with the tailstock, a plug must be made to take the tailstock centre and held in position as shown in SK 2. With a short length of 12mm mild steel in the chuck turn this down until it becomes a close fit in the small hole, that is as far as is possible in such a rough shape hole. Before this can be done, the hole should be cleaned with a round file, just to take of the rough edges, no more. Drill and tap to take the fixing screw, remove, turn round in the chuck and face the other end.

Fit the plug, tighten the fixing screw, mount in the lathe and lightly tighten the chuck in the casting. Turn the lathe by hand and encourage the outer end of the casting to run reasonably true using a gentle tap with a soft hammer or using the method suggested in Chapter 1, Photo 1, do not expect real precision. Again turning the lathe by hand bring a tailstock mounted

centre drill up to the plug just sufficient to mark the plug with the position for centre drilling. Remove the casting from the lathe and after centre punching, centre drill the plug whilst still fitted to the casting, doing this on the drilling machine. Return to the lathe and support with the tailstock centre. Now face the end up to the plug and machine the smaller and larger diameters to their finished dimensions as in **Photo 3**. If you follow the guidelines mentioned above, deep first cut, etc., you should not have any problems. One potential problem though is avoiding the cutting tool hitting the chuck's jaws, ideally a saddle stop should be used to prevent a moment's loss of concentration causing an accident. Otherwise the task will need tackling with extreme caution.

If you look at the photograph closely you will see that it is not a knife tool I am using but what is frequently termed a roughing tool though having mounted its shank at an angle it is basically performing as a knife tool. As roughing tools have not

been mentioned so far, a brief mention here is merited. SK 3 shows the basic differences in shape with roughing tool usually incorporates a larger radius on the tip making it more able to withstand abuse, hence its use for roughing. Also the angle of top rake throws the swarf away from the workpiece when heavy cuts are taken, a task for which it is intended.

Follow this by setting up the top slide fitted with a left hand knife tool as seen in **Photo 2** and machine the angle. This position for the top slide has been chosen as in the more normal position the handle would foul the tailstock. I have to confess that as advised above I started with a substantial cut, at least 2mm deep, but having set the angle a little on the steep side the depth of cut was increasing such that I was going to end up with the diameter at the top rather on the small side. Because of this I turned the top portion parallel to form a neck, this can be seen in a number of the photographs. The situation did though serve to show that the set up quite

5. Supporting the casting with the tailstock centre whilst the steady's arms are set prior to boring

adequately coped with a cut of 4mm depth and would certainly have coped with much more. As I had decided to eventually paint the sloping side I fitted a right hand knife tool and machined a small ledge next to the larger diameter so as to give me a simple edge to paint up to. My error in setting the angle was due to taking a rather glib approach to the task, resulting in me setting the angle unaided. With a little more thought I would have come up with the method illustrated in SK 4.

Having machined the outside there remains the thread to be cut and the base

6. Boring the top of the casting for the threaded insert (see text re change in chuck jaws)

to be machined flat. Remove the tailstock centre, move the saddle to the tailstock end and fit the fixed steady in place, re-engage the tailstock centre and set the steady's arms as seen in **Photo 5**. The small ledge mentioned in the previous paragraph can be seen in this photograph.

It was at this point that I ran into a problem due to the hole provided in the casting not running sufficiently true to enable the thread core diameter to be fully machined. This made me reconsider what it was I was doing and whether this was a good idea for the novice who had probably never, or rarely, cut a thread. The outcome of my deliberations was to bore the end for a mild steel insert which could be threaded prior to being fitted into the casting. If any mishap occurred with cutting the thread it would be a simple exercise to start again.

Photo 6 shows the bore being made but observant readers will note that the jaws in the chuck have been changed for the reverse ones. Having set the fixed steady in preparation for boring for the insert, it would be found that the insert needed to be removed. To accomplish this it is necessary to remove the part from the chuck without disturbing the steadies setting. The normal method of achieving this is to hinge up the top of the steady allowing the part to be removed and replaced at will. Some steadies do not though have hinged tops and in this case the method is to release one arm only of the steady, normally the top one. With the casting removed from the chuck the insert can be removed and the casting returned. Because of the irregular nature of the inside of the casting it would be unlikely to return accurately if mounted again as in **Photo 5** and because of this it is held on its outer

diameter using the chuck's reverse jaws. I would suggest the bore should be 20mm diameter and 15mm deep with the insert similarly dimensioned. Unless you are very confident regarding the cutting of the internal thread, more difficult than an external thread, I would strongly advise this approach.

Next stage is to machine the base of the casting so that it will eventually sit cleanly on the working surface. Whilst if the casting is held on the small end, now machined, a good grip will be possible and

7. Turning the large end plug (note the use of left hand knife tool to avoid problems with fouling the chuck's jaws) used to support the casting whilst machining the base.

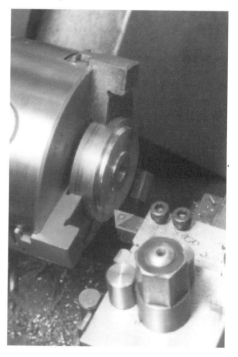

8. Machining the base.

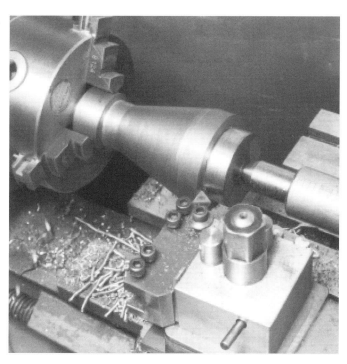

the larger diameters run reasonably true, it will not be sufficiently robust for the base to be machined without additional support. The obvious first answer is to support this again with the fixed steady but in my case it was just too big for the steady I had. As I suspect this will be the case for most, I will detail the alternative .

Place a piece of mild steel in the chuck 45mm diameter minimum and turn a plug to go into the bottom of the casting, it should be sized so that it sits in the hole without any play, very slightly tight would not be a problem. The spigot needs to be in the order of 4mm long and can be seen being made in **Photo 7**. Note the use of a left hand knife tool for machining it, rather than a right hand tool as would seem the obvious

choice. This makes it easier to steer clear of the chuck's jaws. Also drill and tap the centre to take a fixing screw, M6/M8 would be suitable sizes, do not drill completely through but make it a blind hole.

Fit the plug into the end of the casting and using a long screw or a piece of studding, anchor the plug in the casting. Now mount in the 3-jaw chuck as seen in the **Photo 8** and centre drill the face of the plug. Despite the overhang this should be a safe enough operation to carry out but do run at a slow speed as the casting will not be balanced. Now support the end with the tailstock centre and face the bottom of the casting using a right hand knife tool. As the diameter of the plug will prevent machining of the base completely, also

97

reduce the plug's outer diameter until it is only just larger than the hole in the casting, say no more than 0.5mm. Remove the casting from the lathe and the plug from the casting.

You will now find that there is a small rim round the base of the casting where machining has not taken place due to the larger diameter plug. Taking a large half round file and chamfering the inside of the hole will remove the unmachined portion.

Thus far I have detailed the methods but have made no mention of the speeds the machine should run. As has been indicated, machining casting falls into two stages, removing the skin and final machining to size. However, when machining castings, other factors often have to be taken note of, such as intermittent cuts due to irregular shape. In this case, the casting being round, the cut taken will be continuous albeit it may not be a constant depth. As a very rough rule of thumb, I would say the speed for removing the outer skin should be 25% of

the speed when machining free cutting mild steel at the same diameter increasing to 50% once the skin has been removed.

Having machined the casting, the general principles of machining the material have been presented. The considerable variation in shape from casting to casting will though present new challenges in determining how to adequately hold the part. Photo 9 in Chapter 11 is a typical example.

Screw cutting

There now remains the internal and external threads to be cut to complete the jacking mechanism. Screw cutting on the lathe is a rather special subject and will be covered in depth in the next chapter.

Reference 1

The College Engineering Supply. 2 Sandy Lane, Codsall, Wolverhampton, UK. WV8 1EJ tel/fax 01902 842284 E-mail sales@collegeengineering.co.uk

Chapter 10

Jack Continued, screw-cutting

Being of the opinion that articles aimed at the home workshop owner on the subject of screw cutting are very much biased towards using a single point tool and, as this differed from my approach, I was prompted to glance through my library. This confirmed my memory with some 99% of their content based on this form of tooling. Checking the *Model Engineers' Workshop* and the *Model Engineer* magazines over the last ten or so years came up with the same result. These findings have led me to describe my method in greater detail than I had originally intended.

I am not about to suggest that single point tools for cutting threads on the lathe are totally inappropriate but that other methods are now possible. I use the term "now" as almost all the information on the subject seems to be from many years past. The advantage of the single tooth cutter is that it can easily be made in the home

workshop and is independent of the pitch of the thread being cut. It can also be used for any type of thread that uses the same angle.

Using the single point tool

The subject will be discussed in terms of external threads but much of what is written will apply equally to internal threads. Cutting internal threads, and the required shape of the tool, will though have similar problems to those discussed in Chapter 7 in relation to boring.

Using the same single point tool for any pitch assumes that the radius in the root of the thread is ignored and all threads are cut to a point, with only a small radius to strengthen the tip of the tool. This would not affect the thread's ability to mate with its other half, only making the part very marginally weaker which in the majority of cases would be of no consequence. It will be obvious though that the single point tool will be unable to create the radius on the peak of the thread. This would cause problems with mating if the other half was a conventional thread form, such as when making a new part to fit in an existing component, see SK 1.

Two methods of feeding the tool into the workpiece are employed, one to use the cross slide, the other, to use the top slide set at an angle of half the internal angle of the thread. With the first method the tool will cut on both sides whilst in the second it will only cut on the leading edge, see SK 2. With method "B" top rake can be added as shown in SK 3 as it only cuts on the one edge. Setting the top slide angle for method "B" is not easy, especially on some lathes with limited calibration, so an error is understandable. To overcome this it is normal for the angle to be set just short of half, say by 1 to 2 degrees. This results in the major cut being taken off the leading edge but for the right hand to just shave the side thereby achieving a smooth finish. A large top rake will though significantly change the angle of the right hand side and so this would defeat the purpose of the top slide being so set. For this reason a compromise has to be made and rather than the normal 15 to 25 degree rake angle, a rake of about 5 degrees should be employed. This significantly improves the ease of cutting over a tool with zero rake but has minimal effect on the angle of the tool.

Calculating infeed

If you are cutting the outside thread first, normally the preferred, you will not have a mating thread to check it against. Also, as the outside diameter does not change, it is not practical to use this to determine when the thread is at its finished size. For this reason it is necessary to calculate the infeed required. (SK 4)

Setting the tool

There is no point in working to precise angles if the point itself is not set accurately. To do this a thread gauge (front right **Photo 1**) is used as shown in SK 5.

Because of its limitations I would only recommend the use of a single point tool for those pitches and thread angles for which I was unable to get a suitable chaser, likely to be some obscure thread from the past, or present day coarse pitches.

Using chasers

A major factor in the use of single point tooling in the past was surely the expense of purchasing chasers. Whilst commercial chasers are still expensive, and not offered by most suppliers to the home workshop, there are ways round the problem. **Photo 1** shows the tooling that I use consisting of internal and external single point tools, external chasers made from individual die head chasers and internal chasers made from taps. Die head chasers are made in sets of four and if purchased new would be expensive but some suppliers do supply individual chasers cheaply, taking these from used, industrial sets. They are too small to be held on their own but with a holder as seen in the photograph and detailed in SK 6 they can be held with ease.

The design for this is straight forward, just two points being worthy of mention. The clamping force holding the chaser is provided by the lathe's own tool clamping system, the screw in the assembly being there just to hold the assembly together

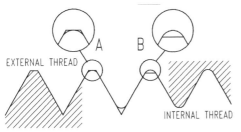

EXTERNAL THREAD

INTERNAL THREAD

AN EXTERNAL THREAD CUT WITH A SINGLE POINT TOOL
WILL FOUL WITH A GUINIUNE FORM INTERNAL THREAD
AS SHOWN AT "A". TO MAKE IT FIT, THE OUTSIDE
DIAMETER SHOULD BE REDUCED AS SHOWN AT "B".

SINGLE POINT AND
FULL FORM THREAD CONFLICTS. SK. 1.

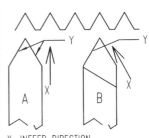

X. INFEED DIRECTION
Y. CUTTING EDGES   SK. 2.

ALTERNATIVE TOOL FORMS

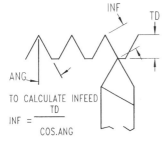

INF

TD

ANG

TO CALCULATE INFEED

$$INF = \frac{TD}{COS.ANG}$$

VALUES FOR "ANG" AND "TD" WILL HAVE
TO READ FROM CHARTS FOR THE THREAD
FORM BEING CUT. NOTE THAT "TD" IS
FROM THE PEAK OF THE THREAD BUT TO
THE POINT CREATED BY THE CONTINUATION
OF THE THREAD FLANKS AND NOT THE
BASE OF THE NORMAL THREAD FORM.

INFEED CALCULATION   SK.4.

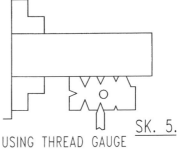

SK. 5.

USING THREAD GAUGE
TO SET THREAD CUTTING TOOL.

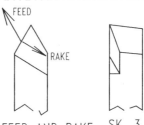

FEED

RAKE

FEED AND RAKE   SK. 3.
DIRECTIONS METHOD "B"

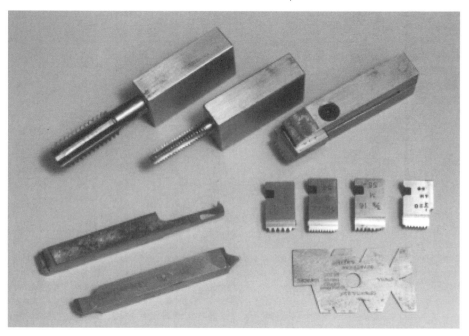

1. A selection of tools for screw cutting on the lathe including modified taps and individual die head chasers.

when removed from the lathe. The countersunk screw head must therefore be below the surface as drawn. Also the height of the step in the upper clamp arm must be just sufficient to ensure that the clamping pressure is applied at the end of the arm thereby providing a secure grip.

Similarly, the taps would be difficult to hold but the simple holder shown makes it easy. Just drill with the drill in a chuck in the lathe's spindle and whilst the holder is held on the top slide, as a result the hole is at centre height. Then drill and tap four holes from below and fit grub screws for holding the tap. Grinding a flat on the tap to aid fixing may seem a good idea but this would prevent the tap from being rotated

to adjust the cutting edge height and angle. Even though the hole is at centre height, some packing may still be required. As is the case with ordinary boring tools, threading tools may also benefit from being a little above centre. It is possible that at smaller diameters the difference in helix angle could cause a problem though I have not been aware of this.

When using chasers it is unnecessary to angle the top slide and infeed is carried out using the cross slide. One major advantage of this and because the thread form conforms exactly to the standard for the thread being cut, the amount of infeed can easily be read from tables. Of course for an external thread the outside diameter

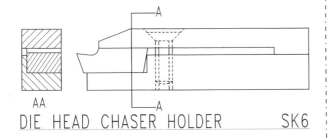

AA

DIE HEAD CHASER HOLDER   SK6

THREADING TOOL
REPLACEABLE TIP   SK8

MODIFIED DIE HEAD
CHASER   SK7

can be measured. In this respect I would suggest that the outside diameter of the part prior to cutting the thread, should be very marginally oversize to allow for the tips of the threads to be fully machined. When turning an internal thread, measuring the diameter is not possible so determining the required infeed and working to this is the only way to proceed. If no other factor overrides the choice, make the external thread first and use this as a gauge to finally check the size of the internal thread being cut last.

Setting the tool is easy, just hold the front of the chaser against the workpiece so that all teeth touch and clamp the tool in place. The tool should only cut on the first few teeth and if there is evidence of the other teeth removing a lot of metal, the tool will need resetting.

At first it may be considered that there will

be no need to shape the tap at all and at larger diameters this will be largely the case. A plug tap will of course be necessary. Earlier in the book when discussing boring small holes, the importance of the shape of the tool was explained and with chasers for small internal threads, the problem is even greater. The reason for this is that the chaser is eventually working at the outside diameter of the thread but the hole in which it is working is still at the smaller core diameter. For this reason grinding away one or more of the unused cutting edges may be necessary, I would suggest though that no more is ground away than is needed. This will leave more of the tap and as a result not make it weaker than is necessary.

Do select a good quality tap for the purpose, preferably ground thread. However, if you are not inclined to destroy

103

a tap in this way, note that car boot sales and market tool stalls often have taps, some new, at very cheap prices. Unless small holes are being threaded choose a larger diameter tap. Typically, for a 20 TPI thread, a 3/8 in. BSF (20 TPI) would be preferred to a 1/4 in. Whitworth (20 TPI)

The common factors

Having dealt in detail with the points that are peculiar to the two methods, there are also common factors.

Having chosen the tool type the first thing to do is to set up the changewheels. If you are fortunate enough to have a screw cutting gear box the situation is very much simpler and needs no explanation. If not then refer to your changewheel chart and set up the gear chain suggested. I use the word suggested as for most thread pitches, in particular the simpler values, say 12, 16, 20, 24TPI, etc., there are many combinations that will come up with the same result. This means that if you are missing a few gears then other suitable combinations are likely with the available gears. Unfortunately, space will not permit detailed explanations as to the way of locating these alternatives but for the simpler threads, observation of the chart and the gears to hand should find a result. Normally, a 20:30 ratio could be replaced by 30:45 if the 20 tooth gear was missing, or 40:60 if the 30 tooth gear was missing.

The formula for the pitch cut is, cut thread = lead screw TPI x Dn1/Dr1 x Dn2/Dr2 x Dn3/Dr3 this is where Dr are drivers and Dn driven gears.

Tumbler reverse

The effect of there being 1, 2 or 3 pairs of gears is that the output to the leadscrew

will reverse depending on the number of pairs of gears, with 2 pairs being reversed from that with either 1 or 3 pairs. This would cause the hand of the thread to be different to that required, most likely a left hand where a right hand is required. However, this rarely causes a problem as the possibility is overcome by the inclusion of a tumbler reverse mechanism between lathe mandrel and the input to the gear chain. This facility is not included on all lathes and achieving the correct hand thread is by the inclusion of an idler gear, that is a single gear between any pair of gears. This in no way affects the ratio of the gear chain and can be any gear that will go in the available space.

Setting up

Setting up the gears is not difficult, albeit not the nicest of tasks. One method of simplifying the set up, is to include between each mating pair a piece of very thin paper to establish an adequate but not over large clearance. The lathe can be turned by hand and the pieces of paper removed before running the lathe under power.

Cutting the thread

With the changewheels set up, the tool of your choice in place and the workpiece in the chuck, thread cutting can begin. Do be aware though that with the ratio of the changewheel gear chain being small the leadscrew speed is not that different to that of the workpiece. If therefore the lathe is run at the normal speed for the diameter being machined, the saddle would traverse at a rapid rate. There is no way that the lathe could be controlled under these circumstances. The lathe must because of this, run at a very low speed and I would suggest the lowest available. As you become confident you may find it possible to move up a speed, or two. These comments assume your lathe has a back gear or some other method of providing speeds of around 50rpm.

If you own one of the lathes that does not have low speed facilities then it will be a case of turning the lathe by hand, this being achieved by fitting a handle at the non-working end of the lathes spindle.

Overrun groove

Only if you turn the lathe by hand, will it be possible to stop the lathe very accurately at the same position at the end of each pass. As a means of providing some tolerance to the final stopping position, a groove is cut at the end of the required thread. Whilst you are in the novice stage, I would suggest that this should be made on the wide side, say three thread pitches. It is in the use of this groove that there is a major difference between using a single and multi tooth tool, but more about that later.

The half nut

A misconception often inferred, if not intended, is that the purpose of the half nut engaging the saddle to the lead screw is to aid screw cutting. This is not so, as its purpose is to enable the saddle to be rapidly moved along the lathe's bed from one position to another unhindered by the leadscrew. Readers who have lathes without half nuts will know the chore of winding the leadscrew to move the saddle from place to place. In fact, whilst slower, cutting threads on a lathe without a half nut would be a simpler task as there would

be no possibility of subsequent cuts missaligning with earlier ones. Let us consider the problem.

If a thread of 8 TPI were being cut on a lathe with an 8 TPI leadscrew, then at whatever point the nut was closed the tool would line up. If however the pitch being cut was 16 TPI, when the nut was closed it would line up with every other pitch on the thread being cut, still satisfactory. With a thread of 12TPI only every other position of the leadscrew would line up with the 12 TPI pitch every other position misaligning, so in this case the half nut can only be closed at certain positions.

Thread dial indicator.

To overcome this, a thread dial indicator is normally fitted which provides indication of when the half nut should be closed. Typically for an 8TPI leadscrew with an indicator fitted with a 16 tooth gear and having four main markings the nut can be closed as follows:

Multiples of 8 (16, 24, etc.) at any position on the leadscrew.

Others that are multiples of 4 (12, 20, etc.) at any of the four main markings, and half markings if provided.

Other even numbers (14, 18, etc.) at any of the four main markings

Odd numbers (11, 13, etc.) at any opposite marking, 1 and 3, or 2 and 4.

Half number (9.5, etc.) at the same position every time

For more complex numbers, say metric pitches on an imperial lathe, or vice versa, the nut should not be disengaged. If you do not have a lathe with an 8TPI, 16 tooth gear, 4 main markings, combination, then see your lathes manual.

Cutting the thread

Wind the cutter up to the workpiece so that it just touches, move the cutter to the right to clear the workpiece and place on a depth of cut using the cross slide and make the first cut. Well, I am afraid that is an over simplification and some preliminary tasks should be carried out before actually making the first cut. I made the comment earlier about there being differences between using a single point tool and a chaser when it came to the purposes of the overrun groove. At the end of the cut there will be two or three ways of stopping it, opening the half nut, stopping the motor and, if available, opening the drive clutch.

Opening the half nut will only be a possibility if a single point tool, (ground in the workshop or a tipped tool, see later paragraph) is being used as with a chaser, some teeth will still be in contact with the workpiece and if this continues to rotate grooves straight round the part will result. However, if a single point tool is being used then opening the half nut is the method to use. You could of course grind away all but two of the teeth on the chaser making it possible to use the half nut with this also, SK 7. Whilst I have never done this myself I am moving towards the opinion that it would be good practice if your lathe does not have a clutch.

Considering now using a full chaser in which case the only option available is to leave the half nut engaged and stop the drive. If a drive clutch is available this is the best way, as with the machine running at a very slow speed it will stop almost instantaneously with very little overrun. If stopping the drive motor is the only option then it will be found that due to the speed of the motor itself and the inertia this creates, the machine will run on after the power has been switched off. Fortunately, with the ratio between motor and workpiece being so high, overrun will be quite small, though it must be allowed for when stopping the machine.

It is because of these factors that I suggested delaying making that first cut, but first doing some dummy runs with the tool just clear so as to become aware of the time intervals involved. This is especially important if the length of thread being cut is short, as the time span will be only a matter of a few seconds, as a result not giving much thinking time. If you do however feel very apprehensive, do consider making that handle for manual operation, after a few threads cut with this you will probably be confident enough to banish it to the "may find another use" box.

It will seem natural to start the lathe, watch the thread dial indicator, close the half nut at the appropriate time, watch the thread being cut, stop the lathe at the end of the thread. This uses the half nut to start the thread and the stop button, or clutch, to stop it. This is not ideal and the following makes it possible for the cutting of the thread to be started and stopped by the same means.

With the lathe stationary, move the saddle towards the tailstock using its hand wheel and watching the dial indicator as this is done. When the dial indicates that the saddle is in the correct position, close the half nut. The traverse of the saddle can now both be started and stopped by the same means, that is, either the start/stop buttons or the drive clutch. This is a much safer procedure. Carry out dummy runs using the procedure and with the chaser just clear of the workpiece doing

2. An almost completely cut thread having been produced with a single point tool.

this until you are 101% confident.

Having arrived at that stage, place on a depth of cut and make your first cut, taking note of the thread dial indicator for determining the half nut closing position. The depth of cut will depend on many factors, typically, material being machined, state of the cutting tool and rigidity of the part being made. I would suggest initially a depth of 0.1mm, gradually reducing this to 0.01mm as the tool becomes deeper in the thread being cut. Keep repeating the process until the thread arrives at a fully formed thread and has the correct outside diameter It will be found that the result is far superior to one cut with a single point tool. Whilst final finishing cuts of 0.01mm will always be the order of the day, you will be able to increase the initial cuts as your confidence grows thereby reducing the number of passes necessary to complete the task.

Internal threads

Cutting internal threads follow exactly the same procedures; use of half nut, method of stopping the cut and the need for a run out grove, unless of course if it is a through hole. Being unable to fully see what is happening, difficulty with clearance between tool and bore, especially at small diameters, does unfortunately make the process a more daunting one. Practice will though increase confidence.

The threaded parts for the jack

With such a detailed explanation given, no more needs to be said regarding the threading operation specific to the parts for the jack. Also by now, with your experience growing regarding plain turning, similarly very little other comment is called for in this respect either. **Photo 2** shows that I did, as a test case, and to provide a photograph, commence the thread with a single point tool and with the top slide set round, though this cannot be seen from the photograph. What can be seen is that the almost finished thread is not that good. **Photo 3** shows the thread having been completed

3. The thread now finished, using a die head chaser, shows a much improved thread. The thread could have been cut fully with the chaser as there is no need to use a single point tool to start the thread.

using the chaser and the difference in quality is obvious. A point to note is that if the part needs supporting with the tailstock a short parallel portion will be necessary to give the chaser room to start, as seen in the photograph.

The diameter of the bore in the insert, seen being made in **Photo 4**, will be equal to the outside diameter minus twice the thread depth, this can be read from suitable thread charts. Also the bore can be increased to the actual thread diameter and to a depth of say 2mm. This will show when the chaser has arrived at the full thread diameter, when the external thread can be used to check if the required fit has been achieved. Finally, **Photo 5** shows the tap being used for the internal thread, that

worked very well after a little problem with shaping the tap for use. It was the first time I had used this tap at such a small diameter and there was not much clearance between it and the core diameter of the thread being made. After realising that the top cutting edge of the tap would have to be ground away to clear the bore the task went without any further problem, in fact I would go so far as to say it was easy.

When you do find it necessary to cut an internal thread using a single point tool, the internal bore will have to be a little on the large size if this is to mate with a full form thread. This is due to the absence of a radius on the crests of the internal thread causing it to foul with the radiused root of the external thread.

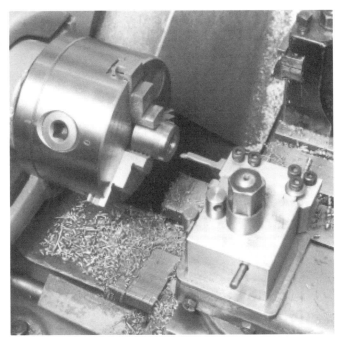

4. A mild steel insert was used for the internal thread rather than threading directly into the casting. This shows the insert being bored.

Imperial pitches

Whilst I work now in metric measurements my main lathe has imperial calibrations and of course an imperial leadscrew. Because of this it would be foolish to attempt to achieve metric pitches when I am making both the internal and external threads. I do therefore produce threads with metric diameters but with the nearest imperial pitch and would expect readers in the same position to do likewise.

Assembly

This needs no explanation other than to say that the insert can be made captive with a little adhesive. As the mating hole in the casting has a base, the adhesive has little work to do other than to hold the insert in place whilst the jack is being moved from

place to place. Castings do also, most of all the unmachined areas, improve in appearance if give a coat or two of paint. I use the smallest sized tin of modelling paint, it is surprising how far one of these tins will go and there is plenty of choice with regard to colours.

Replaceable tip threading tools

A discussion on the subject of cutting threads on the lathe would not be complete without a mention of the latest development, replaceable tipped tooling. These can be obtained for cutting both internal and external threads and at first sight appear to be the equal of the single point tools used in the home workshop over many years. On closer examination, it is seen that not only does the pointed end

5. A modified tap being used to screw cut the thread in the insert.

have the appropriate radius but on either side of the tooth it is shaped to produce the radius on the crest of the thread also, SK 8. Full form threads can therefore be cut with ease and this form of tooling would certainly appear to be the method to use for external threads providing the cost can be justified. However, as the tool cuts the complete thread a separate tip is required not only for each thread form but also for each pitch. Like boring tools for small diameters, threading tools for very small diameters are available but again are particularly pricey.

Faceplate work

In the next chapter we get to grips with using the faceplate, with the project to illustrate this activity being a two wheel knurling tool.

Terms

Back gear. The gear chain associated with the lathe spindle, which when brought into use reduces each of the normal speeds, typically by a factor of 7:1 Used when screw cutting or carrying out heavy or intermittent machining

Die head. An industrial threading device, rather like a very large threading die but with cutting edges that can be removed for sharpening. The device has fitted four cutting edges and these can often be purchased individually from used industrial sets for use in the home workshop as a chaser to be used on the lathe.

Chapter 11

Getting to Grips with the Faceplate

It is easy to lose sight of the real purpose of this chapter believing its aim is to make a two wheel knurling tool. Whilst this is the end product, its main function is to discuss faceplate work with some instructions on knurling to conclude the chapter.

Two wheel knurling tool

This tool should be the standard for use on small lathes as it minimises the load on the lathe's bearings which can be considerable if using a single wheel tool. The design has been established to require faceplate operations and gives plenty of scope for getting to grips with its use as a work holding device. **Photo 1** shows the parts that make up the tool.

Faceplate work

This is the most varied of all forms of lathe work as the shape and size of the parts worked on is far more diverse than that when using a chuck. The task in hand often needs special items to be made to enable the part to be adequately and safely anchored and it is that last aspect, safety, that must have first consideration. With such irregular parts, using a multitude of clamping devices, it is all too easy for one's person or parts of the lathe to foul up with these as they rotate. Because of this, consideration must given to minimising any unnecessary projections. Clamping studs are a major problem as only a limited range is likely to be available and there will be a temptation to use studs that are too long. If this is the case, do cut down the studs to a safer length, I was about to write "a safe length" but realised that no set up on the faceplate is totally safe.

Using suitable clamps is another major consideration, again these should be as small as is possible, yet adequately strong for the task. It is worth noting that a shorter,

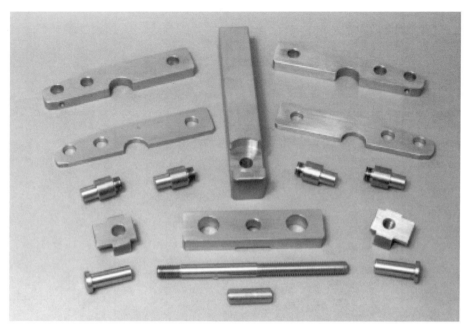

1. The parts that make up the knurling tool with some parts being designed with the use of the faceplate particularly in mind.

smaller cross section clamp, can be stronger than a longer, larger cross section clamp that will more easily bend. Keeping the clamping arrangement more compact will be both safer and more secure. Invariably, a simple stud and bar clamp will require a packing piece under the free end which must be just taller than the part being clamped. Of greater significance in this case, where the clamp is moving rather than fixed as on the milling machine table, is that the packing itself should be captive to the faceplate. It is known for a clamp to become free whilst turning is taking place, the outcome of which is that the piece of packing will be thrown from the rotating assembly with possible serious consequences.

It was with these problems in mind that I developed the clamping system seen in **Photo 2**, and briefly illustrated in SK 1. The set up in the photograph also uses screw clamping dogs. The clamping system consists of a number of parts designed to make it capable of dealing with a range of component heights. Its main feature is that the stud is tapped into the packing piece, making the stud and the packing captive prior to the clamp being applied. With the clamping stud tapped into the packing piece it cannot break free, also, if any one stud would benefit from slight repositioning it can be loosened and moved without parts falling from the assembly. If it is not too big headed of me I cannot rate the system too

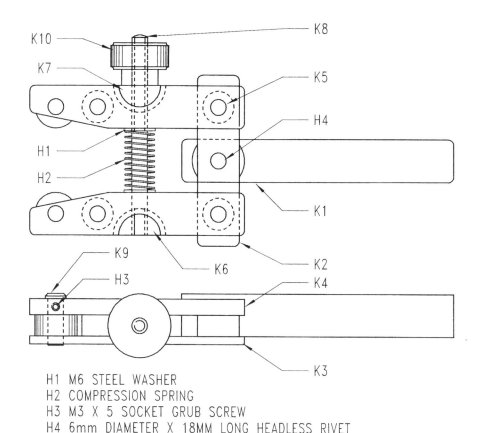

H1 M6 STEEL WASHER
H2 COMPRESSION SPRING
H3 M3 X 5 SOCKET GRUB SCREW
H4 6mm DIAMETER X 18MM LONG HEADLESS RIVET

TWO WHEEL KNURLING TOOL ASSEMBLY

highly as it really does make a difficult operation less difficult.

The clamping dogs will also make a valuable addition to your kit of parts for mounting items on the faceplate One major advantage of these is that they can easily make final adjustments to the position of the part being held. They require little explanation as to the method of

manufacture but making a few will give valuable additional experience in the lathe procedures so far discussed. A point I would like to stress here is do not to be tempted to get by with normal washers even the heavy gauge ones when used with slotted mountings as they are not sufficiently strong. It would be a good idea for a mini project, using a thin piece collet

2. The mounting bar being positioned on the faceplate.

(Chapter 2), to make a quantity of the commonly required sizes, probably M6, M8 and M10 and in larger than normal diameters.

As an aid to security, always use at least three clamps in all but the simplest of set-ups. Also, items that just support the part can be a valuable additional safety feature (see comments re Photos 6 and 7).

Making the two wheel knurling tool
Mounting bar (K1)
Cut a length of 16mm square steel 101mm long and face each end whilst mounted in the 4-jaw chuck to give a 100mm length. Mark out and drill the 6mm hole and use this to locate it on the face plate using the tailstock centre as shown in **Photo. 2**. Closer inspection of the photograph shows the assembly is very much out of balance and if the lathe were run it would vibrate severely. It is necessary therefore to balance up the assembly by the addition of some suitably placed weights. To do this the belt must be freed from the headstock pulley enabling it to rotate as freely as is possible. Add the weights, spin the faceplate, and observe the result, making changes as the test indicates. For relatively light assemblies, tee nuts from the milling

114

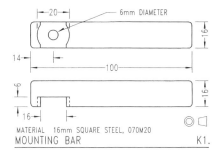

6mm DIAMETER

MATERIAL 16mm SQUARE STEEL, 070M20

MOUNTING BAR   K1.

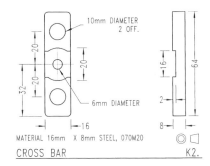

10mm DIAMETER
2 OFF.

6mm DIAMETER

MATERIAL 16mm X 8mm STEEL, 070M20

CROSS BAR   K2.

machine make useful weights as can be seen in **Photo 3**.

One problem with balancing face plates is that even with the belt freed from the pulley, drag from the lathe's bearings can have a significant effect on attaining an effective balance. To overcome this, the dedicated balancing fixture with free running bearings, as seen in **Photo 3**, will enable a much superior result to be achieved, enabling higher lathe speeds to be used.

Having mounted and balanced the assembly, move the cutting tool close into the work and turn the faceplate by hand to see that it rotates without fouling. This is an absolutely essential precaution that must be observed when working with the

3. Using a balancing fixture with free running bearings enables a much superior balance to be achieved compared to balancing whilst mounted on the lathe spindle. A much higher lathe speed can be used as a result.

115

4. Boring the recess in the mounting bar.

faceplate. This is not though foolproof as the saddle and or top slide will no doubt move closer as the work progresses, so do continue to take considerable care.

Enlarge the 6mm hole with a larger drill, say 10mm, to a depth of 5.5mm followed by boring out to 20mm diameter and to a depth of 6mm. However, the cut eventually becomes intermittent as seen in **Photo 4** but providing the tool is sharp and robust the operation should not be a problem.

Cross piece (K2)
This is treated much like the mounting bar but the assembly being symmetrical is automatically balanced, **Photo 5**. Note how the clamping system easily copes with this assembly and at a different height to that in **Photo 2**. Also two clamps are more than adequate for this arrangement.

Arms (K3 and K4)
The four arms are almost identical, but with one pair being thicker. Cut the four pieces,

just over length to allow for finishing, debur but do not machine the ends. Mark out the end 6mm diameter hole position on all four pieces and the remaining holes on one piece only. This is a job for the mini gauge made in Chapter 2 (see Photo 12 in that chapter). Drill the 6mm end hole in all four pieces and then stack them up with a 6mm pin through the four parts. With this done drill the remaining holes as a pack, ensuring as a result that all holes line up. Make another 6mm pin and fit this in the second 6mm hole.

The task now is to make the half round cut-out in the sides of each arm, doing this as seen in **Photo 6**. With this intermittent cut there will be a tendency to move the parts sideways. As a precaution a fence is placed at the underside, just visible in the photograph, to support the arms. By positioning the fence prior to placing the arms, positioning can be achieved

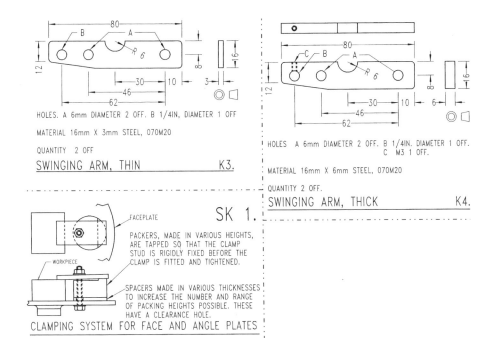

HOLES. A 6mm DIAMETER 2 OFF. B 1/4IN, DIAMETER 1 OFF

MATERIAL 16mm X 3mm STEEL, 070M20

QUANTITY 2 OFF

SWINGING ARM, THIN   K3.

HOLES   A 6mm DIAMETER 2 OFF. B 1/4IN. DIAMETER 1 OFF.
                                         C M3 1 OFF.

MATERIAL 16mm X 6mm STEEL, 070M20

QUANTITY 2 OFF.

SWINGING ARM, THICK   K4.

SK 1.

FACEPLATE

PACKERS, MADE IN VARIOUS HEIGHTS,
ARE TAPPED SO THAT THE CLAMP
STUD IS RIGIDLY FIXED BEFORE THE
CLAMP IS FITTED AND TIGHTENED.

WORKPIECE

SPACERS MADE IN VARIOUS THICKNESSES
TO INCREASE THE NUMBER AND RANGE
OF PACKING HEIGHTS POSSIBLE. THESE
HAVE A CLEARANCE HOLE.

CLAMPING SYSTEM FOR FACE AND ANGLE PLATES

accurately with ease. To do this the centre is placed into the mandrel's taper and, knowing its diameter, spacers of the correct size are used to position the fence. This procedure is seen in **Photo 7**. The spacers being used are the distance gauges made in Chapter 6.

Mount the stack (complete with pins) on the faceplate using the fence as an aid to positioning it, clamp in place and balance. The half round cut-out can now be turned using a suitable boring tool. One problem though exists, it has been explained that a boring tool can only start from a given diameter but in this case it is not possible to drill a hole. It is necessary therefore, before fitting to the faceplate to partially file the cut-out. Commence the

boring operation taking care due to the intermittent cut. As the size approaches 12mm use the 12mm hole gauge (Chapter 5) to check its size, continue enlarging the cut-out until the gauge just drops into the cut-out. As **Photo 6** shows, even with the intermittent cut, a presentable finish can be achieved.

With the pieces still as a pack, mount them on the top slide using the tool clamp and fly cut the tapered end, **Photo 8**. This is a typical case of a task that can very easily be carried out on the lathe, probably more quickly than setting up the milling machine. Similarly, set up the stack so that the ends can be finished using the fly cutter. Make a generous radius on each of the four corners using a file whilst held in the bench

5. Recessing the cross bar. A similar operation to that on the mounting bar but the set up is much simpler and requires no balancing.

6. Making the half round recesses in the arms, note the supporting block just visible below the arms.

7. Using the width gauges, described in chapter 6, to set the position of the arm supporting block just visible in Photo 6.

vice and still with the parts joined as a stack. Finally drill and tap the M3 holes in the two thicker arms.

This completes the faceplate activity and, whilst the essential requirements of safety and security have been well emphasised, the examples are less demanding than will often occur. This of course is no bad thing, being an introduction for the novice. As an example of a much more exacting situation, see **Photo 9**.

Having dealt with the non-turned parts we now turn our attentions to the much simpler turned items.

Arm spacers (K5)

These are outwardly simple items though their manufacture should not follow what would seem the obvious route. Turn one end, part off, reverse in the chuck, turn the second end, as this will not ensure the two ends are accurately in line. With the central part being short it may not return axially in

8. Fly cutting the arms whilst held as a pack on the top slide.

9. An example of a more demanding faceplate assembly than those in this project.

line, see SK 2, especially if the chuck jaws are worn, and normal errors for a chuck of this type will cause errors in concentricity. Of equal significance is that if using the method described above, measuring the length of the central portion, which is quite important, would not be possible whilst in situ.

The method is therefore to use both right and left hand tools to form the part completely prior to parting off. Even with the longer portion being on the inside, this was still too short to permit my micrometer to measure the length of the centre portion. So in the absence of being able to use the micrometer the distance gauges were again made use of as the length of the centre portion is quite critical. The distance of 8mm was made up of 3mm and 5mm gauges but requiring it to be a little over 8mm this was achieved with a piece of thin

paper between the gauges. This should be evident in **Photo 10**.

Swivel pieces (K6 and K7)
The parts that take the adjusting screw, swivel to cope with the change of angle as the tool is opened and closed. Machining these is an interesting exercise. Take two lengths of 16mm x 8mm steel, around 60mm long and hold them as a pair in the 4 jaw chuck to make a 16mm square pack. Use two opposing jaws across the joins and the other two on the 16mm faces, adjusting the jaws until the pack is running reasonably true, precision not a requirement. Again use left and right hand knife tools to turn the two ends prior to parting off. **Photo 11** shows the operation in progress. Before parting off, do check that the diameter is correct for fitting into the half round cut-out in the arms. With the guides parted off two identical parts result, note though that one

10. Again using the distance gauges, this time with their outside fingers, to check the width of the arm spacers.

11. Two pieces of rectangular steel held and machined at the same time to make the swivel pieces.

12. Using the travelling steady to turn a piece of 1/4 in. bar down to 6mm for making the adjuster stud.

requires to be tapped M6 whilst the other is drilled 6.2mm diameter. Generously deburr all around and two more parts are finished.

Adjuster stud (K8)

It had been my intention to bypass the use of the travelling steady. However, not having any 6mm diameter steel to make this stud, and not wanting to wait for a delivery, it created the need to turn down a length of 1/4 in. material. This could only be done satisfactorily using a travelling steady that gave me the opportunity to take a photograph for publishing.

The purpose of the travelling steady is to support a part, usually long relative to its diameter, which is too weak to support itself whilst being worked on. It may be that the part cannot be supported at its outer end using a tailstock centre or even if it can, is still insufficiently strong for the machining required. In this book we can only deal with the simple task to be carried out here, in any case this is the most likely application.

Using the travelling steady is probably simpler than one may expect. Place the material in the chuck running true within 0.02mm total indicator reading and, with the steady fixed and adjacent to the chuck, the arms are adjusted. At this stage the material must only project from the steady's arms by a few millimetres, say 8mm. Using the cross slide to achieve the required diameter, turn a length of about 5mm using the top slide, the tool is now about 3mm from the steady's arms. If you are unfamiliar with the travelling steady, it is fixed to the saddle and moving the cross slide does not change the steady's position. Do not move either the cross slide or the top slide but move the saddle back sufficient to turn the length of the part required. Now move the material out from the chuck, sufficient to make the part and machine it traversing the cutter using the saddle, and the task is complete, **Photo 12**.

If the part to be made is too large a diameter to pass through the lathe's mandrel, the initial setting up will have to be done using a small off-cut. Quite heavy cuts are possible using a travelling steady

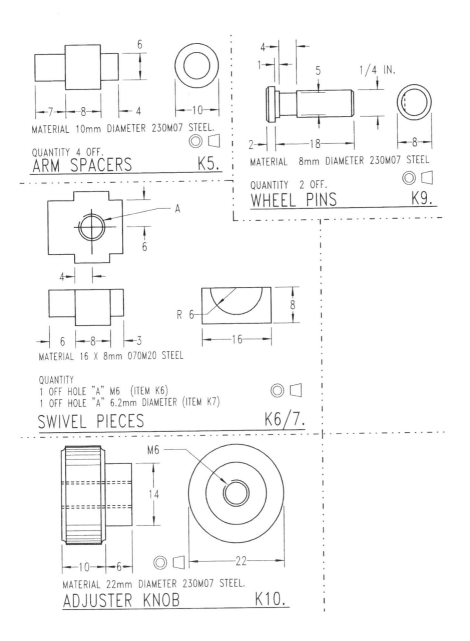

6

7 8 4

10

MATERIAL 10mm DIAMETER 230M07 STEEL.

QUANTITY 4 OFF.

ARM SPACERS K5.

4
1
5
1/4 IN.

2 18 8

MATERIAL 8mm DIAMETER 230M07 STEEL

QUANTITY 2 OFF.

WHEEL PINS K9.

A

6

4

6 8 3

R 6

8

16

MATERIAL 16 X 8mm 070M20 STEEL

QUANTITY
1 OFF HOLE "A" M6 (ITEM K6)
1 OFF HOLE "A" 6.2mm DIAMETER (ITEM K7)

SWIVEL PIECES K6/7.

M6

14

10 6

22

MATERIAL 22mm DIAMETER 230M07 STEEL.

ADJUSTER KNOB K10.

123

and it is the aim normally to finish the machining at one pass. It is also essential that the tool is kept feeding, as it is the cutting action that keeps the workpiece in contact with the steady's arms. With this in mind it is worth noting that the operation prefers a heavier cut, reducing a diameter by a small amount may not generate sufficient force to keep the workpiece against the steady's arms. Similarly, if the feed is stopped a small groove in the workpiece will result. If you need to reduce the diameter of the available material using the travelling steady, or if you have the correct material to hand, it is a simple task to thread the stud from either end using the die holders made in Chapter 7. Even if you have the correct 6mm diameter material it would be a good idea to start with a piece of 8mm turning it down to 6mm using the travelling steady. This will give you experience in using the device.

Apart from the adjusting knob there remain only the knurling wheel pins and a rivet pin, these are quite straight forward and now with your expertise increasing, no explanation regarding making these is necessary. Just one point is worthy of comment regarding the wheel pins. These, as detailed, are made from 230M07 mild steel, if you anticipate much use of the tool making them from silver steel and hardening them will be a good policy. Even so, they are simple to make and if made from mild steel will be easily replaced if eventually wear becomes excessive.

Assembly

Deburr all the parts and generally clean up the surfaces. Lightly countersink the holes where riveting is to take place also the inside of the holes as the knife tools are

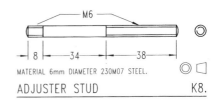

MATERIAL 6mm DIAMETER 230M07 STEEL.

ADJUSTER STUD   K8.

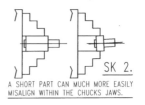

A SHORT PART CAN MUCH MORE EASILY
MISALIGN WITHIN THE CHUCKS JAWS.   SK 2.

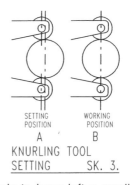

SETTING   WORKING
POSITION   POSITION
A   B
KNURLING TOOL
SETTING   SK. 3.

likely to have left a small radius in the corners of the arm spacers. Also the recesses in the mounting bar and the cross bar need opening up to 16mm wide at the edges so as to enable the two parts to fit together. Only a little has to be removed so can easily be done using a file. Proceed slowly checking to make sure a close fit between the two parts results. Assemble and lightly rivet checking that all appears

13. The knurling tool getting its first task, making its own adjuster nut, hence the plain nut fitted.

OK and that the arms move freely, if so complete the riveting and file the heads flush for appearance's sake. Fit the stud with swivel ends, washers, the spring, and an M6 nut temporarily and the tool is ready for use.

The adjusting knob (K10)

As yet we have not discussed the knurling wheels themselves. The tool takes wheels 5/8in. diameter by 5/16in. wide and with a 1/4in. bore, you will though have to decide the forms of knurl you wish to produce, that is, straight or helical, and the pitch of the teeth produced. Most suppliers refer to the pitch as fine, medium or coarse whilst a few will actually quote the pitch in terms of teeth per given length. The decision will depend on the type of work probable in the workshop, but if workshop equipment is to

be a major feature then medium knurls will be the one to start with. If funds will run to it I would suggest both straight and helical, if not then just the straight versions but of course the choice is yours.

Knurling, the method

Having made your choice and the knurls purchased knurling can commence. Knurling is a relatively simple task now that you have the correct tool for the job but like all tasks on the lathe, there are some rules that need observing. You will be forgiven for considering that the knurl is made by forcing the wheel into the workpiece, creating the knurl by a metal forming. Experienced writers on the subject will tell you that in fact the action is to cut the teeth. This is certainly true as small fragments of metal will result indicating

125

14. A knurled part direct from the knurling tool has rough edges to the knurl. In this photograph the ends of the knurl are being finished with a small round nose tool. This gives a better result than using left and right hand knife tools.

some form of cutting action. Forming does also occur as, if the part is measured when the knurl is fully formed, the outside diameter will be found to have grown, indicating that some limited forming has taken place. Of course, if the knurl is further fed in, the outside diameter will reduce to the original material diameter and even smaller as more metal is cut away.

Place a short length of 22mm diameter steel in the chuck, drill and tap M6 and turn the reduced diameter portion and we are ready to knurl the main diameter. Place the knurling wheels so they overlap the right hand end of the workpiece by no more than 2mm and with their centres just forward of being exactly in line with the centre of the workpiece, as seen in SK 3A. Close the wheels onto the workpiece and, with the lathe turning, move the cross slide forward

so as to line up wheel and workpiece centres SK 3B. This providing the initial depth of cut, the knurl can now be formed by traversing the tool slowly to the left, wind the tool back so that it almost disengages the wheel from the work and deèpen the cut a little and make a further cut. Repeat this until a full knurl is achieved. **Photo 13** shows the operation under way. Knurling should be carried out at a slower speed than normally used at the diameter being worked though there is no need to use very slow speeds, for this at 22mm diameter I would suggest around 100 rpm.

This is one operation where a good flow of coolant is a very definite plus as it will carry the small fragments of metal away some of which would otherwise be pressed into the knurled surface by the knurling wheels, thereby reducing the quality of the

15. The complete two wheel knurling tool.

result. Unfortunately, pumped coolant is unlikely to be a facility available to many, so, having arrived at the last cut, stop the lathe and brush away with a wire brush all the metal fragments from the wheels and the workpiece. At this stage I use an oil can with some very light oil that I pump on as the final traverse is made resulting in most of the fragments being carried away. A small tray on the cross slide catches the oil avoiding the lathe becoming unnecessarily dirty.

The leading and trailing edges of a knurl thus far produced are unlikely to be acceptable and will need some cleaning up. Using left and right hand knife tools is possible but this gives for me a rather abrupt transition, I prefer using a small round nose tool as seen in **Photo 14** that gives a much more acceptable result.

With the knurling complete the adjuster knob can be parted off, reversed in the chuck holding it on the reduced diameter and the end faced. The knob is then complete and can replace the temporary nut on the knurling tool that now becomes another finished project as can be seen in **Photo 15**.

Milling/drilling spindle

In Chapter 12 we get to grips with a milling/drilling spindle that gives plenty of opportunity for trying out your new found skill of cutting threads, together with plenty of external and internal turning. In all, this will move you from the novice to the knowledgeable learner stage, and is followed in the final chapter with a milling cutter chuck. This is a major project that should move you well towards the status of an experienced turner.

Chapter 12

Mill Drill Spindle

Having, through the chapters to date, attempted to move the novice turner through to a capable beginner, we finish with two sizeable and complex projects. However, if you have attempted successfully at least most of the projects thus far, there is no reason why these items should not be within your capability.

Production schedule

In Chapter 1, I stated that becoming a capable centre lathe operator was more than conquering the task of applying the cutting tool to the workpiece but of more significance is the choice of tool, workholding device, and the sequence of operations leading up to a completed component. For that reason I am detailing only the manufacturing sequence as by now you should have conquered the task of metal removal.

Bearing clamp nuts (3). Cut two pieces 45mm diameter 16mm long. Fit reverse jaws. Grip the first piece. Machine end face.

Reverse part in chuck. Face to a length of 15.2mm, bore 20.5mm and counterbore 24mm, 3.2mm deep. Repeat for second part making sure the bores are the same diameter as they are to be mounted on a common stub mandrel.

Make a washer 23.5mm diameter 3mm thick and drilled 6mm Place a piece of steel, say 30mm diameter, in the 3-jaw with about 25mm length projecting. Turn a stub mandrel, 10mm long and a close fit in clamp nut bores. Centre drill, drill and tap M6. Do not remove from the chuck! Fit the first clamp nut. Reduce diameter to 37.1mm making the head to its finished length of 7mm. Skim outside to 44mm diameter. Make grove adjacent to head. Make thread to 37mm diameter. Face end to achieve length of 8mm Chamfer both sides of head and leading edge of thread. Repeat for the second nut ensuring both threads have the same outside diameter, **Photo 1**. Lastly, drill the holes used for tightening the nuts on final assembly.

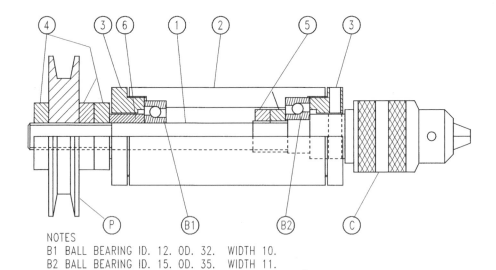

NOTES
B1 BALL BEARING ID. 12. OD. 32. WIDTH 10.
B2 BALL BEARING ID. 15. OD. 35. WIDTH 11.
BOTH BEARINGS EITHER "SINGLE ROW DEEP GROOVE"
OR "SINGLE ROW ANGULAR CONTACT"

C DRILL CHUCK WITH 1/2IN. X 20 TPI INTERNAL THREAD MOUNTING.

P PULLY TO SUIT SPEED OF DRIVE MOTOR AND SPINDLE SPEED REQUIRED.

MEDIUM DUTY MILLING DRILLING SPINDLE.

Body 2. Cut one piece 45mm diameter 91mm long. Fit in chuck (large 4-jaw if available). Centre drill, drill and tap end M8. DO NOT face the end as projection from chuck is probably too great. Remove, reverse and centre drill end. Remove, fit an M8 hexagon head screw in tapped end. Fit 3-jaw chuck. Grip head of the screw. Support with the tailstock centre. Finish the outer diameter to 44mm.

Return the 4-jaw. Remove the hexagon head screw and fit part protecting it from damage. Set part to run true using a dial test indicator as precision is important in view of the steady being used to support the part. Fit and set steady. Drill with a large size drill, **Photo 2**. This will cause considerable heat to be developed so do check that expansion does not cause the steady to become over tight. If this happens the lathe will stop abruptly as the steady will act as a brake. Face, just sufficient to achieve a clean end. Bore to 35.5mm and 9mm deep. This is just larger than core diameter for a 20 TPI Whitworth form thread. If you use a different thread form and/or pitch you will have to calculate the required bore diameter. This comment also applyies to other internal threads required later. Make 3mm grove at base of bore.

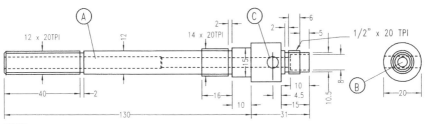

NOTES
HOLES   A. 6mm   B.   5.2mm   C.   6mm
DEPTH OF HOLES "A" AND "B" CAN VARY DEPENING ON LENGTH OF DRILLS AVAILABLE.

12mm DIAMETER TO BE A LIGHT PUSH FIT IN THE BALL RACE TO BE FITTED

15mm DIAMETER TO BE A CLOSE SLIDING FIT IN THE BALL RACE TO BE FITTED

MATERIAL. 20mm DIAMETER 230M07 STEEL

SPINDLE   Pt1.

1. The thread being cut on the Bearing clamp nuts.

Above :2. Drilling a large hole through the Body ready for final boring.

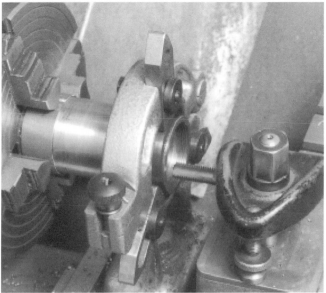

Left: 3. Making the internal thread in the Body.

132

*4. Boring the bearing
housing in the Body*

Make thread, **Photo 3**. Bore 32mm diameter by 8mm deep for bearing housing, **Photo 4**. Remove steady, and body from chuck. Reverse part in chuck placing the faced end against chuck face. Set to run true. Refit steady. Face to a length of 90mm, measure off the chuck face. Repeat as first end, but note the differing bearing housing diameter. Bore through to 26mm , **Photo 5**.
Spindle (1). Cut one piece 20mm diameter 162mm long. Fit 4-jaw chuck. Fit material. Adjust to run true at the jaws. Fit and adjust steady adjacent to the chuck. Move steady to end. Centre drill 8mm diameter. Drill 5.2 diameter, see drawing re depth. Release one arm of steady. Remove part taking note of the two chuck jaws opened. Reverse and fit into the chuck using the same two jaws. Reset the steady arm. Centre drill 9mm diameter. Drill 6mm diameter hole.

Fit centres and drive plate. Set up part between centres. Rough turn three diameters to plus 0.5mm and length to 130.5mm Turn groves at end of threaded portions. Finish each diameter in turn taking note of the accuracies required at the same time finishing the 10mm and 16mm lengths. Make 12mm thread. Make 14mm thread, **Photo 6**. Fit half centre. Face to 130mm long and chamfer.

Reverse the part between centres, protecting the 12mm thread from the driving dog screw using copper sheet. Turn the 0.5in. diameter making the 20mm diameter 16mm long. (You may need to change the 1/2 x 20 TPI thread to suit a differing chuck mounting, but take note of the requirements for using the collet.) Turn the 10.5mm diameter making the 0.5 in. diameter 10mm long, **Photo 7**. Make the grove at the end

133

5. Boring the through hole in the Body.

6. Making one of the external threads on the Spindle.

7. Preparing the Spindle outer diameters for mounting the drill and collet chucks.

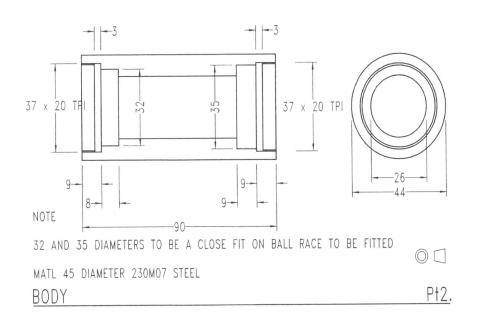

37 x 20 TPI

37 x 20 TPI

3

3

32

35

9

8

9

9

26

44

90

NOTE

32 AND 35 DIAMETERS TO BE A CLOSE FIT ON BALL RACE TO BE FITTED

MATL 45 DIAMETER 230M07 STEEL

BODY   Pt2.

135

12 x 20 TPI

7

—|7|— |—30—|

NOTES 1 HOLE 5.2 DIAMETER

MATL 30 DIAMETER 230M07 STEEL

QUANTITY 3 OFF REQUIRED

BEARING ADJUSTMENT NUTS Pt4

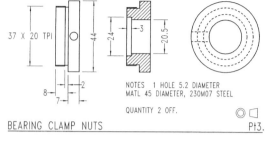

37 X 20 TPI

44

24

3

20.5

8—| |—2

7—| |—

NOTES 1 HOLE 5.2 DIAMETER

MATL 45 DIAMETER, 230M07 STEEL

QUANTITY 2 OFF.

BEARING CLAMP NUTS   Pt3.

14 X 20TPI

7—| |— |—25—|

NOTES   1 HOLE 5.2 DIAMETER

MATL 25 DIAMETER 230M07 STEEL

QUANTITY 2 OFF REQUIRED

BEARING CLAMP NUTS   Pt5

12

|—16—| |—20—|

MATL 20 DIAMETER, 230M07 STEEL

12mm TO BE CLOSE SLIDING FIT
ON SPINDLE

QUANTITY 1 OFF.

BEARING ADJUSTMENT TUBE Pt6

of the thread. Make 1/2 in. x 20 TPI thread. Very lightly skim over 20mm diameter for appearance sake. Lightly chamfer ends. Fit half centre and face end to 15mm length.

This manufacturing sequence serves to show a major advantage of turning between centres and which is often the reason for adopting the method. That is, concentricity can so easily be achieved, even when the part is removed and rotated end on end, or removed for checking its fit with other components. However, for absolute concentricity it is essential that the headstock centre runs perfectly true. This is easily achieved by fitting a soft centre that can be machined on the lathe prior to the workpiece being fitted. This machining out the effect of any minute errors in the lathe spindle bore, the centre itself, or this having been fitted

with less than clean surfaces.

Bearing adjustment nuts (4), bearing clamp nuts (5). It is essential that the faces of these nuts are parallel, if not, bending of the spindle may result when they are tightened.

Cut three pieces 30mm diameter 8mm long and two 25 diameter 8mm long. Fit into the 3-jaw against the chuck face and drill 8mm, ream if you have a suitable reamer. Repeat. Drilled holes are often smaller where they break through. If so, the parts will need lightly countersinking on that face to avoid problems with fitting the parts to the taper stub mandrel.

Fit a length of 10mm and make a taper stub mandrel to hold the nuts using their 8mm bores. If you need to recap regarding taper stub mandrels see Chapter 5 SK 5. Fit first part. Face the

136

outer end. Remove nut. Reverse. Refit to the stub mandrel. Very lightly face the already machined end using a left hand knife tool. Face the right hand end to a length of 7mm Stop the facing cuts just clear of the mandrel. Repeat for remaining parts. Remove the mandrel and fit each nut in turn into the chuck, as when drilling the 8mm hole. Open up to 10mm to remove the small unmachined portion in the centre.

It will be safer and easier to bore and thread the nut if held at the outer end of the chuck's jaws. However, there is a limit as to how narrow a part can be safely held

9. Making the threads in one of the Bearing nuts.

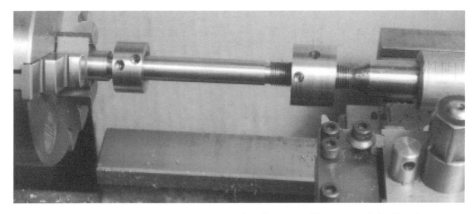

10. Using the spindle as a mandrel for machining the outer diameters of the Bearing nuts.

in this way, hence the use of thin piece collets in some cases. Seven millimetre can though, at these diameters, be held adequately but it is difficult to ensure the part is running true. Using the front end of the tailstock mounted drill chuck gets over the problem. Place the part in the chuck and lightly tighten, advance the drill chuck up to the part and push the part very slightly into the chuck and tighten the chuck fully, see **Photo 8**. Rotate the chuck by hand and observe that the part remains in contact with the drill chuck for a complete revolution, if not, repeat process.

Fit the first nut (Part 4). Bore 10.5mm diameter. Make internal thread, **Photo 9**. Repeat for two remaining nuts. Similarly, repeat sequence for the two nuts (Part 5), this time the bore is 12.5mm diameter.

Drill holes in nuts. Fit and lock onto the spindle. Fit 3-jaw. Protect the spindle and grip on major diameter. Support outer end. Skin outer diameter of nuts, **Photo 10**. Chamfer available edges. Reposition nuts so that remaining edges can be chamfered. This sequence illustrates a feature that is

often beneficial. That is, that a part already made can be used to hold other parts for machining, both on the lathe and similarly on the milling machine. Do not lose sight of this fact.

Bearing adjuster tube (6). Again it is essential that the two ends are parallel and true to the bore.

Cut a piece of 20mm diameter, 17mm long. Fit into the 3-jaw. Face one end. Remove and reverse. Face to 16.3mm long. Drill and bore 12mm diameter, close sliding fit on the spindle. Make a 12mm taper stub mandrel. Fit the adjuster tube. Use left and right hand knife tools, face both ends to achieve 16mm length. Skim outer diameter to improve appearance. Lightly chamfer ends.

Collet chuck body (7). Cut a piece of 20mm diameter, 27mm long. Fit in the 3-jaw. Face the end. Centre drill. Drill through 10mm diameter. Bore through 10.5mm, close fit on spindle. Bore 11mm diameter 11mm deep. Bore 0.5 in. diameter 3mm deep. This must be a close fit on the drill chuck mounting, you may need to make a

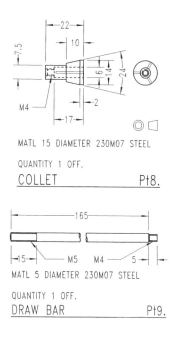

MATL 15 DIAMETER 230M07 STEEL

QUANTITY 1 OFF.

COLLET   Pt8.

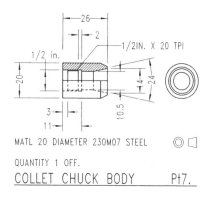

MATL 20 DIAMETER 230M07 STEEL

QUANTITY 1 OFF.

COLLET CHUCK BODY   Pt7.

MATL 5 DIAMETER 230M07 STEEL

QUANTITY 1 OFF.

DRAW BAR   Pt9.

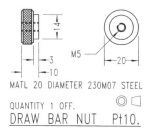

MATL 20 DIAMETER 230M07 STEEL

QUANTITY 1 OFF.

DRAW BAR NUT   Pt10.

plug gauge to check this. Make groove at base of thread. Make 1/2 in. x 20 TPI thread, use spindle to check size.

Fit 4-jaw chuck. Grip spindle on 12mm thread, suitably protected. Fit steady in a position to support spindle on its major diameter but with arms apart. Engage tailstock centre. Adjust 4-jaw such that 12mm diameter close to the chuck runs true. Set the steady. Remove tailstock centre.

Fit collet chuck body to the spindle, Skim over outer diameter. Face end to give 26mm length. Set top slide and produce outer taper (**Photo 11** shows that I did this operation later mounted in the 3-jaw chuck) Set top slide to 12 degrees. Bore collet internal taper to 14mm diameter, **Photo 11**. Leave top slide set at this angle.

Spindle (1) (continued). Remove collet body. Now that there is no further need to support the spindle with the tailstock centre, the 8mm x 10mm deep bore can be made, **Photo 12**.

Collet (8). The collet requires completely machining at the one visit to the chuck to ensure concentricity. Place a length of 15mm diameter in the 3-jaw, about 30mm projecting. Rough turn all the outer diameters. Centre drill and drill 5mm 17mm deep. Drill and tap M4. Turn 7.5mm diameter using left and right hand knife tools. Turn major diameter to 14mm Finish turn the taper portion. Bore the 6mm

139

11. Again using the spindle as a mounting . This time for the Collet chuck body when machining its internal taper, thereby ensuring that it runs true when eventually mounted on the spindle in use.

12. With the spindle still mounted in the lathe its final internal bore is made.

140

13. Boring the collet.

diameter, **Photo 13**. Part off to 22.2mm   A saddle stop, as seen in **Photo 13**, set to the appropriate depth would be an advantage to the operations taking place in both Photos 12 and 13. Make a taper stub mandrel to hold the collet on its 6mm bore. Fit the collet. Face end to 22mm

It remains for the collet to be slotted but to avoid lengthy repetition of the method observe the method I have adopted

for the collets in Chapter 13. I did though for this collet use a holder made out of hexagonal material, giving three rather than four slots.

The collet assumes that you will be using mini mills with a 6mm shank, collets with other bores can of course be made as are required.

The complete set of parts can be seen in **Photo 14** which includes also the draw bar

14. The completed set of parts.

(9) and draw bar nut (10). For these I think the drawings will give adequate information for them to be made.

Assembly

Assemble the parts temporarily. Spot through the hole in the front bearing nut (3) marking the position for the hole in the major diameter of the spindle. Dismantle, Drill the spindle 6mm diameter. This permits a bar to be used to lock the spindle for removing the chuck and making adjustments at the pulley end. Dismantle, clean all parts thoroughly and assemble finally. Adjust to the point where end float just disappears.

Drive assembly

As the requirements for the power transmission assembly will be dependant on local conditions I have not described this in detail. Such factors as type and speed of the drive motor, the machine on which it is to be used, in particular the tee slot spacing, will have considerable bearing on the arrangement. **Photo 15** shows my assembly in its prototype stage, still in need of tidying up, guards, finish, etc. The motor is that from a small double ended grinder that runs at a nominal 3000rpm and being

142

15. The drive assembly in its prototype stage.

an induction motor holds speed very well under load. These are an economic source of a suitable motor, and have the added advantage of an on/off switch.

SK 1 shows how the spindle is mounted onto the base plate and how the position of the hexagon head screws seen in **Photo 15** are positioned to line up with the tee slots in the cross/vertical slide of the lathe.

Pulleys

The likely choice of material for the pulleys is aluminium which to date in this series has not had a detailed mention. Providing free machining aluminium is obtained,

machining the material is very easy. Normal practice is for aluminium to be machined at a higher speed than for steel, say twice the speed, and with the tool having a greater top rake angle of around 25 degrees.

Cut a piece of aluminium for each size of pulley to be made, I am not quoting sizes as these will depend on the speed of the motor, type of belt, duty the spindle is to be put to, etc. Fit reverse jaws to the 3 jaw and fit the first blank. Face end, remove, reverse and face second end to thickness required. Bore hole to size required. Make a stub mandrel to fit the bore and with an M8 tapped hole. Fit pulley using a

143

substantial washer and M8 screw. Using parting off tool, or some other grooving tool, rough out groove. Set round top slide to angle required and with a left hand knife tool finish the right hand flange. Remove pulley, reverse, refit and finish other flange, **Photo 16**. Skim over outer diameter and remove sharp edges.

Using the spindle

Uses for the spindle will be many and varied as has been seen with similar devices featured over the years in the *Model Engineer* and *Model Engineers' Workshop*

magazines. **Photo 17** shows a small spindle having a keyway milled into it using the roughly completed drive assembly. The power transmission method you use will be up to you. However, it is not uncommon for the motor to be mounted separately and for the spindle to be driven from an overhead shaft. This has advantages in that the smaller spindle assembly would be easier to mount at the working position.

Materials

It has been my practice in recent years to make sure that I obtain freely cutting steel to specification 230M07 (or EN1a, very

16. Turning one of the Pulleys.

144

SK1.

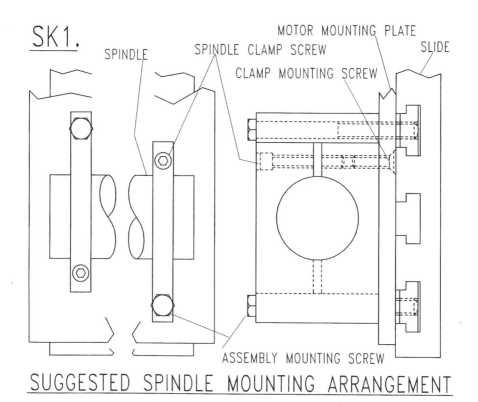

SUGGESTED SPINDLE MOUNTING ARRANGEMENT

17. The spindle being tested using the prototype drive assembly.

146

similar) However, I decided for this project to test the leaded versions of these (230M07 Pb / EN1a Pb) which machine even easier and found this to be a noticeable improvement. The free cutting aluminium was to BS4300/5 2011T3. This I found very easy to machine.

The Ball Bearings I fitted were single mounting angular contact bearings, the sizes of which are quoted on the assembly drawing. As an alternative to the angular contact bearings, which are more expensive, single row, deep groove bearings, could be used. These are made with the same dimensions but have reduced, axial load capabilities. They should though be adequate for the average home workshop use.

Milling cutter chuck

In the next and final chapter the subject is a milling cutter chuck. This again provides a substantial turning project to get to grips with. With both these final projects completed satisfactorily, you will have no need to consider yourself a novice any more.

Chapter 13

A Milling Cutter Chuck

One of the earliest lessons a novice, milling machine operator will learn is that the spiral action of an end mill will, when taking a cut, attempt to draw the cutter from the chuck holding it. The result is that it soon becomes apparent that the drill chuck usually supplied with the average mill drill is quite inadequate. Having purchased my first mill drill for around £600 I soon learnt that this was so but was dismayed to learn that a suitable milling cutter chuck was going to set me back in excess of £100. This seemed quite disproportionate compared to the cost of the machine and I was led to consider making one. This I did and the resulting chuck has been more than adequate over the 15 years of use. I have though found that I would like to use endmills having a greater shank diameter than the 1/2 in. or 12mm that my chuck catered for. I therefore made a version to suit 16mm diameter and this is the chuck

featured in this chapter. Whilst economy milling cutter chucks can now be had one that covers up to 5/8in./16mm and provides for both metric and imperial sizes with plain and threaded shanks would still cost serious money.

I will, as I did for the mill drill spindle in the last chapter, limit my text to a production schedule format, expanding on this only where considered necessary.

Taper and chuck body (1)

Set the top slide for eventual machining of the taper using the method described in Chapter 8 but in this case the smallest end is nearest to the chuck. Leave the top slide set at this. The drawings and the following text are for a number 3 Morse taper, if you require another taper some dimensions will need changing.

Cut one piece 136mm long 32mm diameter. Fit securely in the 3-jaw. Centre

149

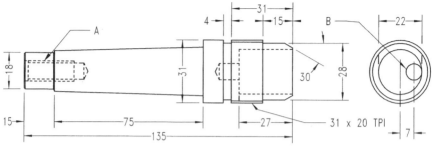

HOLES
A. TAP TO SUIT DRAW BAR
B. 8mm DIAMETER X 10 DEEP

MATERIAL. 32mm DIAMETER 230M07 STEEL

TAPER AND CHUCK BODY   1.

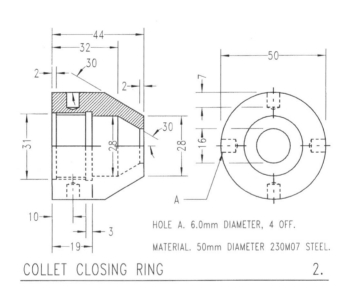

HOLE A. 6.0mm DIAMETER, 4 OFF.

MATERIAL. 50mm DIAMETER 230M07 STEEL.

COLLET CLOSING RING   2.

1. Preliminary turning the taper portion of collet body, parallel at this stage.

2. Finishing the Morse taper.

3. Above: Cutting the thread on the collet body.

4. Left: Setting steady whilst the body is supported by the tailstock centre

5. Boring the collet body.

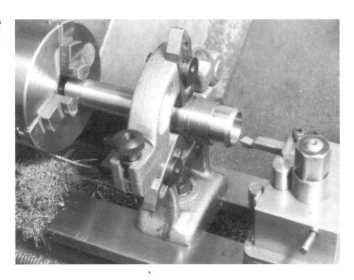

drill end to 6mm diameter. Support with tailstock centre. Face end as close to the centre as the tool will permit. Finish turn 18mm diameter 15mm long. Chamfer end. Reduce to 25mm over 75mm **Photo 1**. Disengage centre. Fit steady at outer end of 25mm diameter. Engage centre. Set steady. Remove centre. Drill and tap to suit the draw bar to be used.

Release one arm of steady. Move steady nearer to the chuck. Remove part, reverse and grip part on 18mm diameter, suitably protected. Move steady to outer end of 25mm diameter and reset the one arm. Centre drill outer end to 10mm diameter.

Remove steady. Engage tailstock centre. Rough turn outer diameters. Turn taper, finishing with a round nose finishing tool. Remove and check in the taper in which it is to be fitted. Having used the method described in Chapter 8 this should be a formality. Return to the chuck and again support with the tailstock centre. The part

must now remain in the chuck until machining is complete. Once more skim over the taper with the finishing tool, **Photo 2**. THIS IS ESSENTIAL to ensure that it is running true again. Finish machine 31mm outer diameter. Finish machine the 28mm diameter making the 31mm diameter 30mm long. Machine the 4mm groove.

Machine thread, **Photo 3**. Remove tailstock. Fit steady in position to support the 31mm diameter. Re-engage centre. Set steady, **Photo 4**. Remove tailstock centre. Face end to give 15mm length. Turn small taper. Drill with large size drill 25mm deep. Bore to 22mm diameter, 27mm deep, **Photo 5**.

In Chapter 1, I referred to the need for parts to be designed with the method of production in mind. This chuck body is a perfect example. The short parallel piece next to the threaded portion serves no purpose in the final design. However, without it there would be nowhere for the steady to support and making the part

6. Making the small bore of the collet closing ring.

7. Threading the collet closing ring.

8. Making the internal taper in the closing ring. Note the boring bar is fitted upside down for machining at the rear of the bore. This enables the top slide setting to be used for both the closing ring and the collets themselves ensuring identical angles.

would be much more of a problem.

Remove from the lathe and drill the 8mm diameter hole on the drilling machine. **Collet closing ring (2)**. Cut one piece 50mm diameter 45mm long. Fit reverse jaws in the 3-jaw and fit part. The part must not be removed from the chuck until all boring / threading operations are complete. Face end. Skim outer diameter for appearance sake as far as the chuck jaws will permit. Centre drill. Drill 15mm or as large as is available. Bore through 16mm diameter, **Photo 6**. Bore 28mm diameter (close sliding fit on 28mm diameter on chuck body) 32mm deep. Bore 29.5mm (this assumes 20 TPI Whitworth thread form) 19mm deep. Bore 31mm diameter 2mm deep. Make 3mm wide groove. Make

thread, **Photo 7**.

Set the top slide to 30 degrees. Fit boring tool, upside down to machine on the back of the bore. Turn the internal taper, **Photo 8**. Make sure transition between 28mm diameter and the taper maintains the 32mm dimension. Leave the top slide set at this taper until collets are completed.

Remove part and drill tommy bar holes. Return to the 3-jaw, suitably protected. Face end to give 44mm dimension. Turn outer taper.

Collets (3). Take a length of 25mm diameter say 300mm long and place in the 3-jaw. Use the 4-jaw if your 3-jaw is not sufficiently accurate. Fit steady adjacent to the chuck and set jaws. Move steady to 50mm from end of bar for machining the

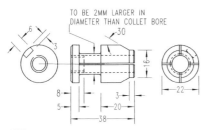

TO BE 2MM LARGER IN
DIAMETER THAN COLLET BORE

NOTES
THERE WILL BE NO 3mm PROJECTION ON THE 16mm AND
5/8 COLLETS 20mm DIMENSION WILL BECOME 17mm AND
38mm WILL BECOME 35mm

MATERIAL 25mm DIAMETER 230M07 STEEL

SLOT COLLET WITH AVAILABLE SLITTING SAW,
1mm TO 1.5mm WIDTH PREFERRED.

THE THREAD IN THE COLLET BORE IS 20 TPI WHITWORTH
FORM, FOR BOTH IMPERIAL AND METRIC SHANK
DIAMETERS. MAKE THIS A VERY FREE FIT ON THE CUTTER
SO THAT ONLY THE COLLET JAWS ESTABLISH THE
POSITION OF THE CUTTER IN THE CHUCK, THEREBY
ENSURING CONCENTRICITY OF THE CUTTER HELD WHEN
IN USE.

COLLETS   3.

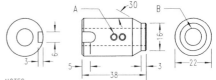

NOTES
THERE WILL BE NO 3mm PROJECTION ON THE 16mm AND 5/8
HOLDERS 38mm WILL BECOME 35mm
HOLES
A. M4 2 OFF, POSITION TO SUIT CUTTER. SEE SEPARATE DRAWING.
B. DIAMETER TO SUIT CUTTER

MATERIAL 22mm DIAMETER 230M07 STEEL

HOLDERS, LARGE DIAMETERS.   4.

HOLES
A. M4. 1 OFF ONLY,
       POSITION TO SUIT CUTTER. SEE SEPARATE DRAWING.
B. DIAMETER AND DEPTH TO SUIT CUTTER.
C. M6
       MATERIAL 22mm DIAMETER 230M07 STEEL

HOLDERS, SMALL DIAMETERS.   5.

9. Making multiple short parts in this way avoids finishing up with many short stubs if parts are individually held in the chuck.

10. Turning the collet grove.

first collet, **Photo 9**. Face end. Centre drill and drill, just smaller than the bore of the collet being made. With a drill, 1.3mm smaller than the bore of the collet being made drill to a total depth of 42mm. This is about 0.2mm larger than the core diameter of the thread eventually to be cut. Machine 16mm diameter and the 30-degree taper. Machine groove, **Photo 10**, diameter depending on bore of collet being made. I used a triangular tipped tool for this so the groove has sloping sides. Bore the collet making it a close fit on the cutters to be held. Machine the outer diameter to 22mm to be a close fit in the collet body. Part off at 38.2mm length. Move the steady back towards the chuck and make the next collet.

Using a 4-jaw chuck (unless your 3-jaw is very accurate) fit the first collet,

protected, and adjust to run true. Face end to a length of 38mm. Lightly chamfer end. Make thread, free fit on endmill thread, using a single point tool, **Photo 11**.

Cut a piece of 20mm square about 50mm long. Fit 4-jaw and fit piece of metal making it run reasonably true. Face end. Centre drill and drill, say 12mm diameter, and 6mm deep. Bore to 22mm diameter, 5mm deep, **Photo 12**. Drill and tap M5. Using available scraps of material set up guides for positioning collet and fit suitable slitting saw in the chuck, **Photo 13**. Make the first slot. Remove collet with holder, rotate 90 degrees and make the second slot. Repeat for slots 3 and 4, **Photo 14**.

Using the same basic set-up but with collet raised with additional packing, make cut-out in base of collet using a 6mm

11. Above: Making the thread in the base of the collet.

12. Left: Making a fixture for holding the collets for slotting, see photos 13,14 and 15.

13. Setup for locating collet holding fixture, see photo 14.

Below: 14. Collet being slotted.

15. Using the same holding fixture for making the cut-out in the base of the collet.

16. Boring the "C" spanner.

160

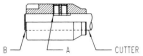

B ——| |—— A |—— CUTTER

POSITION THE TWO GRUB SCREWS SUCH THAT THE ONE
NEAREST THE BASE OF THE HOLDER IS AGAINST THE END
OF THE FLAT(A) ON THE CUTTER, WHILST THE END OF THE
CUTTER IS JUST OUTSIDE THE END OF THE HOLDER (B).

THIS ENSURES THAT THE CUTTER CAN NEITHER MOVE IN
OR OUT OF THE HOLDER WHILST HELD BY THE COLLET
CLOSING RING.

GRUB SCREW POSITIONS
LARGE DIAMETER CUTTERS.

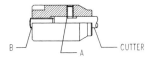

B ——| |—— CUTTER
          |—— A

POSITION THE HOLDING GRUB SCREW SUCH THAT IT
IS AGAINST THE END OF THE FLAT(A) ON THE CUTTER,
WHILST THE END OF THE RESTRAINING GRUB SCREW
IS JUST OUTSIDE THE END OF THE HOLDER (B).

CHOOSE LENGTH OF RESTRAINING SCREW TO SUIT

FOR 6mm DIAMETER SHANK CUTTERS THE HOLDING
SCREW WILL HAVE TO BE POSITIONED ON THE
TAPERED PORTION OF THE HOLDER, SEE DRAWING
FOR PART 5.

THIS ENSURES THAT THE CUTTER CAN NEITHER MOVE
IN OR OUT OF THE HOLDER WHILST HELD BY THE
COLLET CLOSING RING.

GRUB SCREW POSITIONS
SMALL DIAMETER CUTTERS.

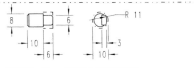

MATERIAL. 10mm DIAMETER 230M07 STEEL.

COLLET LOCATING PEG   6.

LOCATING PEG FITTED INTO HOLE
IN BORE OF THE CHUCK BODY.

FILE VERY SMALL NOTCHES AROUND
TOP CORNER OF LOCATING PEG AND
MAKE CAPTIVE BY CENTRE PUNCHING
CHUCK BODY ADJACENT TO THE NOTCHES.

COLLET LOCATING PEG ASSEMBLY

FIX PIN AND HANDLE USING ADHESIVE,
RESIN TWO PART SUGGESTED.

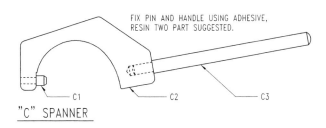

C1 ——| |—— C2 |—— C3

"C" SPANNER

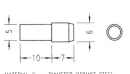

MATERIAL 6mm DIAMETER 230M07 STEEL.

DRIVE PIN   C1.

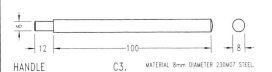

HANDLE   C3.   MATERIAL 8mm DIAMETER 230M07 STEEL.

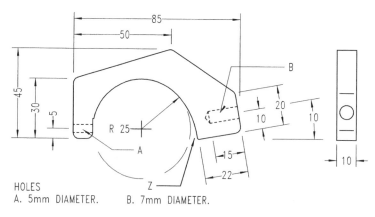

HOLES
A. 5mm DIAMETER.   B. 7mm DIAMETER.

NOTE
Z. SHAPE TO ENABLE SPANNER TO FIT COLLET CLOSING RING.

MATERIAL. 45mm X 10mm 070M20 STEEL

"C" SPANNER BODY   C2.

endmill, **Photo 15**. Using a drill chuck for holding milling cutters is in general not acceptable practice due to the spiral action of the cutter pulling the cutter from the chuck. However, at 6mm as in the photograph, there should be no problem providing the cutter is sharp and feed rate is kept low.

Understandably, you may question the use of collets and other parts made from unhardened steel. I can though from experience confirm that they will give adequate service over many years in the home workshop if used with care.

Holders (4 and 5). Make these following the same procedures, where appropriate, as used for the collets. Take note of the comments on the drawings regarding positioning of holding screws. These holders are not slotted. Dimensions for the

positioning of the holding screws are not given as I am not sure that the position of the flats on the endmills are standardised from make to make.

Collet Locating Peg (6). Place a piece of 10mm diameter in the 3-jaw. Reduce diameter to 8mm over a length of 10mm Lightly chamfer end. Part off at 16mm overall length. Shape end of peg, by hand if necessary. Fit into collet body.

"C" Spanner. I will only detail the major points regarding making this item.
Cut a piece of steel for the Body (C2) mark out the centre position of the cut-out and centre punch. Before making the cut-out, drill hole "A" making sure it is in line with the centre point of the cut-out.

Fit faceplate and position body on this using the tailstock centre in the centre punched impression and clamp

162

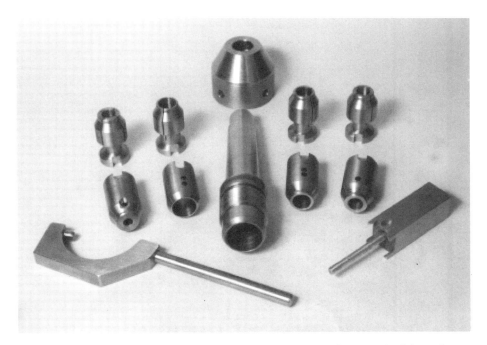

17. The finished kit. For a full range of metric and imperial collets to suit plain and threaded shanks many more collets would be required.

in place. Place a piece of thin card between body and faceplate to avoid the boring tool damaging the faceplate as it breaks through. Balance faceplate assembly. Centre drill and drill 10mm diameter. Bore to 25mm radius, **Photo 16.** Using a saddle stop is recommended for this operation as it will prevent the tool accidentally contacting the faceplate. Shape. Drill hole "B". Make other parts. Assemble.

The completed kit

Photo 17 show the completed kit, excepting at the time I had not finished the 16mm threaded shank collet. Incidentally, at this shank diameter cutters can be had up to 20mm diameter. Readers who wish to use the full range of both imperial and metric cutters will require even more collets, in which case the saving over even the cheapest chuck will be considerable.

Put to the test

I was confident that the chuck would work satisfactorily with threaded shank end mills, as with these any turning of the cutter in the collet has the action of pulling the collet forward into the closing ring thereby holding the cutter even more firmly. Holding a large, plain shank cutter was though an unknown quantity. I therefore made my first task a heavy cut taken with a 16mm plain shank cutter. The 6mm by 4mm wide cut, seen

18. Taking a heavy cut (6mm x 4mm) using a 16mm plain shank cutter fitted in a holder rather than a collet. The chuck performed perfectly.

being taken in **Photo 18** was taken at a fairly high feed rate without any sign of complaint. I am confident therefore that the chuck will perform without problems, not only with threaded shank cutters but also with large plain shank ones.

For the newcomer to using threaded shank cutters the following is the method of fitting them into the collet. Fit collet into the chuck body and fit collet closing ring running it down until it just contacts the collet. Screw in the cutter and continue turning until the end of the cutter contacts the bottom of the bore in the chuck body. Loosen the closing ring very slightly and again turn the cutter so as it again contacts the bore in the body. Hand tightening of the closing ring is all that is required. This process ensures that the cutter is definitely in contact with the chuck body and that it will remain in the same axial position even if the cutting load causes the cutter to rotate as mentioned in the previous paragraph.

The cutting edges of a milling cutter can be VERY SHARP, especially when new. Do therefore wear a glove, or use a piece of thick cloth, when screwing a cutter into its collet, as it is so easy to cut one's fingers. This can be particularly a problem if the cutter is a little tight in the collet.

In conclusion, I do hope that you have found reading this book beneficial and that you will be able to make at least most of the items featured. If you do I am sure that you will feel much more confident regarding your abilities when using the centre lathe, the machine at the centre of most workshop projects.